"The process of biblical improvised. But what d[...] book, Lauren Whitman path between those two associated with each stage of counseling. Full of practical examples that vivify these major tasks, Lauren's book is an ideal resource for training lay counselors and for use in graduate biblical counseling programs."

> **Michael R. Emlet,** Dean of Faculty and counselor, Christian Counseling & Educational Foundation (CCEF); author of *Saints, Sufferers, and Sinners: Loving Others as God Loves Us*

"The moment I finished *A Biblical Counseling Process*, I added it to our counseling training program. Rightly interpreting people's experience has often been a far more difficult task for biblical counselors than rightly interpreting the text of Scripture, and Lauren's work raises our ability to accurately and helpfully understand the people God places before us."

> **Nate Brooks,** Assistant Professor of Christian Counseling, Reformed Theological Seminary, Charlotte, NC

"Lauren captures the principles for thoughtfully and wisely walking alongside a hurting individual. She demonstrates how each stage builds on each other, along with practical illustrations and examples. It is a wonderful resource for those looking to better understand the process of counseling."

> **Julie Lowe,** Faculty and counselor, Christian Counseling & Educational Foundation (CCEF); author of *Building Bridges* and *Child Proof*

"We listen better, empathize more accurately, and offer more helpful guidance when we have a process we trust. Lauren provides clear tasks and manageable assessments for the beginning, middle, and end of the counseling process. Whether you are a new counselor learning the ropes or an experienced counselor reviewing the basics, *A Biblical Counseling Process* will help you structure your thinking as you serve as God's ambassador to those coming to you for counsel."

> **Brad Hambrick,** Pastor of Counseling at The Summit Church, Durham, NC; general editor for *Becoming a Church that Cares Well for the Abused*

"While I have counseled for thousands of hours, I sometimes struggle when trying to describe the particulars of the counseling process to my students. Lauren Whitman's book fills this need as she describes the particulars of the process of counseling. As I read, I often found myself saying, 'Yes, that's how we do it.' I anticipate that this resource will benefit many as we strive to faithfully shepherd the souls of God's people."

> **Jim Newheiser,** Director of the Christian Counseling Program, Reformed Theological Seminary, Charlotte, NC

"This slim volume is a weighty resource. Lauren Whitman's outline of the process of biblical counseling is methodical, giving a structure and a reason to follow it. It is biblical, rooting that method in Scriptural truth. It is practical, with examples that ground us in real life. New counselors will find a pattern to help them begin. Experienced counselors will find many fresh insights. This outstanding resource fills a significant gap in our biblical counseling library."

Steve Midgley, Executive Director of Biblical Counselling UK; senior minister of Christ Church, Cambridge

"While most counseling books give you principles and stories, this one is unique because it teaches you the important parts of a counseling process. But it does this in a gospel-centered and practical way that I haven't seen often. If you are a counselor, your knowledge of how to help your counselees will grow considerably, your use of Scripture will be strengthened, and your hope in Christ will be made more firm. Who could ask for more? This book taught me much, and it will also teach and edify you!"

Deepak Reju, Capitol Hill Baptist Church, Washington, DC; author of *On Guard*; coauthor of *The Pastor and Counseling* and *Build on Jesus*

"Reading *A Biblical Counseling Process* will help shape you into a better counselor and provide you with direction toward more effective counseling sessions. With a focus on knowing the person rather than solving a problem, this book offers distinctly biblical direction coupled with well-defined, compassionate applications of professional practices. An excellent primer for formal construction of the counseling process from start to finish."

Eliza Huie, Director of Counseling, McLean Bible Church, Vienna, VA; dean of biblical counseling at Metro Baltimore Seminary; coauthor of *The Whole Life*

"Biblical counseling is nuanced work, and I've often wondered if I'm doing it right. Thankfully, what Lauren has written here is both intuitive and practical. She answers questions I didn't even know I had about the process, and then offers examples from counseling conversations. Counselors of all experience levels will benefit from reading this book. I'll be keeping it nearby for quick reference and session prep!"

Christine Chappell, Outreach Director and *Hope + Help Podcast* host, Institute for Biblical Counseling & Discipleship; author of *Help! I've Been Diagnosed with a Mental Disorder* and *Help! My Teen is Depressed*

A BIBLICAL COUNSELING PROCESS

GUIDANCE FOR THE BEGINNING, MIDDLE, AND END

Lauren Whitman

New
Growth
Press

newgrowthpress.com

New Growth Press, Greensboro, NC 27401
newgrowthpress.com

Cover Design: Faceout Books, faceoutstudio.com
Interior Design and Typesetting: Gretchen Logterman

ISBN: 978-1-64507-190-7 (Print)
ISBN: 978-1-64507-191-4 (eBook)

Library of Congress Cataloging-in-Publication Data on file

LCCN 2021022836 (print) | LCCN 2021022837 (ebook)
LC record available at https://lccn.loc.gov/2021022836
LC ebook record available at https://lccn.loc.gov/2021022837

Printed in the United States of America

28 27 26 25 24 23 22 21   1 2 3 4 5

To Chad:

I can no longer tell where I end and you begin…
I could not have written this book without you.

I love you.

CONTENTS

Introduction

THE PURPOSE AND SCOPE
OF THIS BOOK

This is a small book with a focused purpose. The content works together to address the following three broad "what" questions for the beginning, middle, and end of the counseling process:

- What does the process focus on at each stage?
- What should I consider at each stage to maximize the help I'm offering?
- What might each stage look and sound like in a counseling case?

These questions are explored in the context of an adult who has voluntarily sought out individual counseling. The questions are considered in a way that highlights biblical priorities, and they are specifically for counselees who desire their counselor to work from a Christian perspective.

The process I describe is what we're aiming for—and therefore doesn't account for how things do not always go the way we would hope in counseling. Sometimes people end counseling prematurely; sometimes they drop off, and you hear from them two years later; sometimes they feel that their counselor isn't a good fit; sometimes you refer them elsewhere because you feel you aren't the right fit. Any of these outcomes can happen—and are common within the counseling field! But this book will help you do what you hope to do with a willing counselee who remains committed to the process.

To capture the process in a big-picture way, I have identified two major tasks for each phase of it. You will find that all of the chapters in each of the book's three parts work together to explain, describe, support, and illustrate these major tasks. Surely, there are dozens of tasks that go into the work of serving as a counselor, but I chose two primary tasks for each stage in order to focus on providing an overview of the entire process. However, I have compiled a list of resources at the end of the book that point you to some of the topics that I did not cover or alluded to only briefly.

I've written the book's guidance from the vantage point of my service at the Christian Counseling & Educational Foundation (CCEF), which is a nonprofit, fee-for-service counseling center. Though I hope what I share will also be helpful for a pastoral counseling session in a church, or even for talking with another church member over coffee, the book is primarily intended to help those who work as counselors in a formal setting. For this reason, the process I will describe has an end to it because it assumes that people won't remain in your life, but instead that you will have come alongside others for a season to offer help for their specific needs.

Why read a book about a biblical counseling process? To grow in skillful love. To call ourselves biblical counselors, we aim for nothing less than to love others from a pure heart, a good conscience, and a sincere faith (1 Timothy 1:5). There-fore it is appropriate, it is beneficial, and it is fitting to pursue resources that help us grow in the applied, biblical wisdom we rightfully want to offer those we counsel. If people reach out for our help, we want to be ready to respond and offer the fruit of our skills and training. This practical book intends to add to your training so that you can increase in skillfulness. It intends to add to your training so that you can grow in how you show God's love to your counselees.

Chapter 1

WHAT IS A BIBLICAL COUNSELING *PROCESS*?

Before we begin exploring the phases of the counseling process, we must define our terms. If you have picked up this book, my guess is that you already have a working definition in your mind of *biblical counseling*. Here's mine: biblical counselors believe that the life, death, and resurrection of Jesus Christ is not only the turning point of human history but also has supreme relevance for people's lives today. Jesus is alive, reigning now in heaven, interceding for his people, offering real-time help through his Spirit—and biblical counselors habitually consider who Jesus is because we have faith that he speaks pointedly and intimately to all aspects of human experience. The Bible speaks to our joys, sorrows, sins, hopes, fears, and desires, and we endeavor to handle God's Word with deft and skill, to handle it in a way that spurs people toward greater trust, obedience, and worship of God, no matter what they are facing. To do this, we consider together God's good words; we discern together what wisdom looks like in light of God's good words. We explore how we, as followers of Christ, can bring the vivaciousness and verve of his counsel into how we live our everyday lives.[1]

We will spend a bit more time now fleshing out what a biblical counseling *process* is because "process" runs the risk of abstraction and, therefore, can be less helpful. For our counseling process to be biblical, I will propose two defining characteristics.

A BIBLICAL COUNSELING PROCESS IS *PERSONAL*

The word *process* sounds stiff and wooden. But the process is personal because biblical counseling endeavors to connect the person of Christ to the person we are meeting with. In revealing himself to us, by making his invisibility visible (Colossians 1:15), God has been personal with us. He wants us to know him as he is. He wants us to receive him into our lives and to be in communion with him. And so we can anticipate that he will be personal with our counselees. God comes to each of us personally—he stands at the door and knocks—again and again, repeatedly, daily, over a lifetime. He always sees our needs, always knows our hearts, always lives to provide for us. And his Word—a living and active Word—speaks personally. How will his living Word direct and guide as he draws near to our counselees in their struggles? Biblical counselors will have the privilege to see how the Lord does this in an up-close and personal way.

As God speaks and ministers to us, he invites us to make ourselves known to him, just as he has made himself known to us. And herein we find one goal of our counseling. Any kind of counseling aims to help people grow in self-understanding—a valid endeavor that we'll discuss later—but biblical counseling

---

1. For a detailed, full-orbed description of biblical counseling, see the Biblical Counseling Coalition's confessional statement at biblicalcounselingcoalition. org/confessional-statement/.

also encourages people to take what they have come to understand about themselves and share it with their God. Counseling conversations help people better know their hearts *and* pour out their hearts to God (Psalm 62:8). We want to help people connect personally with God, to not only pray but to know what it is to dwell in the shelter of the One in whom they live, move, and have their being (Acts 17:28).

Additionally, the process is personal because you are there! God made you a unique person, and he has called you to bring yourself—your heart, your personality, your story, your experiences—into the counseling room for the blessing and benefit of your counselees. Who are you in the counseling room? You are in a role, to be sure. The role is counselor, and the person you are meeting with has sought you out to play this role. There are certain boundaries and guardrails with this role, and those are good and important to maintain.[2]

Regardless of the specific professional boundaries you implement, it is important to remember that people are helped by genuine relationships, not the role. So biblical counselors are personal with people in ways that are appropriate to the kind of relationship we are in. This means that you should be you. For example, you are being personal in counseling when you say, "I am not quite following you. Can you say a bit more?" because you really can't follow and you're glad to say so if it means you gain clarification that you would have otherwise missed. You are being personal when you let yourself tear up because you really are moved by what this counselee is telling you. You are being personal when you show your anger because this person has been

---

2. For example, I don't share my personal phone number with counselees. They can reach me through formal channels—at my work email address or by calling the front desk and leaving a message with the receptionist. Depending on the context in which you counsel, and your personal preferences, these boundaries and guardrails will differ.

harmed by an injustice, and it really doesn't sit well with you. Again, people are helped by people, not by the role. Who we are—what we think, how we feel, what we're bothered by, what delights us—is what we want to freely bring with us into our counseling. Making ourselves known in the counseling room is surely not the focus of the counseling, but neither is it irrelevant.

Why we've become a biblical counselor is also relevant. We are not in the counseling room just because we really like helping people (though we do like that!). We are there on behalf of another Person. Because Jesus has won you over, his mission and his good purposes in people's lives have become your mission. Thus the counseling process is also personal because God has been personal with you. He has worked in your life. And part of his work has led you into the counseling room.

What are you there to do? Metaphors can help here. Ed Welch writes, "There is typically a dominant metaphor—a picture—that shapes our care for other people. . . . The possibilities include shepherd, brother, sister, father, mother, friend, priest and scores of others."[3] One metaphor that has shaped my care for people lately is that I am an *ambassador* for Jesus in the counseling room.

An "ambassador" may not have initial appeal because it sounds formal. But my conception of it very much coincides with a counseling process. By definition, an ambassador is an official representative, and I draw the word from the apostle Paul (see 2 Corinthians 5:20). In his letter to the church at Corinth, he affirms that Christians—those whose lives have been changed by Christ and now bear his name—are to represent the God who saved them. Therein is the connection that inspires me: How am I representing Christ in the counseling room? How

3. Ed Welch, "Counselor as Host," *CCEF* (blog), August 4, 2014, https://www.ccef.org/counselor-host/.

am I making God and his ways appealing to this person? This is personal because representing the person of Christ requires that I know him for who he is, know what he says, and know what he is like. If I don't know him well, I cannot represent him in my responses, words, comfort, encouragement, and exhortation. Therefore, one of my tasks as an ambassador is to intimately know the person of Christ so that I can represent him well. The way I personally represent him is distinctly "Lauren" because I, too, am a person, but it is the Lauren who is a worshiper of Christ, who is being transformed and recreated into the image of Christ. Somehow, as Jesus recreates us into his image, we become more uniquely ourselves, and this is who we want to authentically be when we counsel.

Thus, as you read the suggestions and guidelines in this book, you should be actively considering how you, specifically, will enact them. How do they intersect with your unique gifting, skills, training, and approach to biblical counseling?

A BIBLICAL COUNSELING PROCESS IS *ADAPTABLE*

This point builds off the first. If our process is personal, then it must take the counselee into account at every juncture. That requires us to adapt our counsel to the true concerns, fears, desires, and struggles of each individual. We do not invite people to enter into a preformulated program when they come to counseling. Instead, we want to respond to the actual needs on the ground. To do that, we must get to know this individual. We must reject our own tendencies to generalize and make assumptions about people. To be personal, we ask questions. We follow up. Biblical counseling is an exploratory process that unfolds over time. We are humble; we don't know what we will discover, but we want to know. And as we hear from people, as we learn about what is on their hearts, we are spontaneous, quick on our feet, willing and ready to consider and reconsider, to circle back, to clear up misunderstandings—*to adapt*—all based on what we're hearing in real time.

Many Christian authors have pointed out the adaptability of Jesus's ministry. Jesus was—in the most positive sense of the word—unpredictable in his responses to people. Although he was unpredictable from our perspective, of course he possessed complete knowledge and understanding of a person's heart. He knew where each person's struggles really were, and he responded accordingly. We don't have his same level of insight into people's hearts. But we can pursue it. Proverbs 20:5 is a favorite verse among counselors. It tells us, "The purpose in a man's heart is like deep water, but a man of understanding will draw it out." We want to be men and women of understanding who can skillfully draw out what is in the hearts of the people we counsel. Adaptability is required for carefully handling the deep waters we draw from a person's heart. We respond to what is actually there—not what we think is there.

To summarize, a biblical counseling process is personal. We represent the personal God as we pursue knowing and loving people as they are and meeting them where they are. And as an outworking of being personal, our counsel adapts to people as unique individuals as we contextualize God's Word to the particulars of their lives. These two principles undergird the guidance that follows in this book.

Let me draw your attention also to the word *guidance* itself. This word is in the book's title, and it fits well with what we've covered so far. Guidance is not prescriptive. It is not a set of rules that must be strictly followed. Rather, guidance provides tracks to run on, but, to extend the metaphor, as a counselor you have to determine how fast to go on the tracks, when to make stops, when to pull over, when to change directions, and when to call for backup. All of these adaptations are based on the individual you're meeting with and your discernment of what will best meet the needs of the moment.

Part 1:
The Beginning of the Counseling Process

The primary focus of the beginning of the counseling process is to build your relationship with your counselee. Two major tasks will help you accomplish this:

1. Coming to know the person and their concerns accurately, and
2. Earning the person's trust by showing a kind of care that embodies the love of Christ.

Chapter 2

BUILDING A COUNSELING RELATIONSHIP

Chapter 1 built the case for a biblical counseling process that is personal, as well as the idea that people will be helped most when we as counselors are personal with our counselees. In this chapter, we will think more deeply about the counseling relationship itself. Why do this? It is widely established in counseling research and studies that the relationship between a counselor and a counselee is influential in bringing about positive changes in the counselee's life, and that a counselor's empathy for the counselee is an especially important ingredient within that influential relationship. Even more than evidence in counseling literature for the importance of the counseling relationship, our Christian faith intuitively leads us to similar ideas. So let's now think biblically about the topics of the counseling relationship and the counselor's expressions of empathy so that we can be encouraged and motivated in how we build relationships with those we counsel.

To begin, let me first acknowledge that some readers might be wary of the word *empathy*. I want to be clear that empathy does not mean we are in blind agreement with someone and accept his or her perspective as the true perspective. Rather, empathy simply aims to accurately understand someone's perspective and experience. I don't want us to reject this idea because we are skeptical of the word. There is a strong biblical basis for the idea. Therefore, I will offer a working definition of empathy that demystifies the word and captures the idea. Then I will back it up with biblical support.

Empathy is an outworking of love and it says, "I see you and that you are struggling. I am committed to not standing far off from you, just as Christ does not stand far from you. I will work hard to understand you, your experience, and your perspective because I want to know you."

To love like this, we pattern ourselves after Christ, because it is the Word becoming flesh and dwelling among us that captures *empathy*. By entering into our world and becoming like us in our humanity, in our frailty and vulnerability, Jesus put himself in our shoes (John 1:14). He didn't stand far off from us when he saw us in our helpless estate, but he was moved by our sin-filled, sorrow-filled experiences and took up the mission of our salvation. He did this because he understood very well what we were facing. He knew our circumstances, our helplessness, and our fate, and he responded—at great cost to himself. He was so willing to identify with us that he became one of us. Even now he sympathizes with our weaknesses because he has taken on flesh. He knows what it's like to live in a world with fallen, sinful people. He knows what it's like to be tempted (Hebrews 4:15). He practiced perfectly how to turn to the Father in faith and obedience, which now makes him a perfect intercessor for us (Hebrews 7:25). He knows what we need.

As his people who are now being remade into the image of Jesus, we also are called to enter people's lives in ways that echo his incarnational love (John 13:35). We humbly enter into people's stories, cultural understanding and experiences, emotions, and narratives, seeking to really understand what this person's life is actually like. We ask questions. We eschew assumptions. God knows us truly. We seek to know others truly. If we fail to come to know people accurately—that is, if we fail to empathize truly with their experiences—then we will miss the opportunity to come alongside them in ways that are most helpful because we won't be speaking knowledgeably. If we can't or won't enter into the person's world, we will "miss" what is most important to the person and therefore miss the opportunity to have the kind of impact we'd hope to have. If we don't come to accurately understand both what is happening and the person's experience and perspective of what is happening, then how can we help guide them? Empathy helps to lay the groundwork for effective influence.

So to build a relationship where you steward your influence well, you aim to inhabit this person's world, which is an act of humility that reflects and is reminiscent of Jesus humbly entering our world (Philippians 2:5–8). Because of how God made us, we are drawn to those who take the time to care about what we are facing and put in the effort to understand us. Empathetic movements in counseling build the person's trust in you. And trust builds the relationship, which leads us to our next point.

As we consider the counseling relationship we are building with counselees, what biblical support can capture *why* the relationship is of critical importance? Here's a description of the nature of the relationship, followed by biblical support.

To enter into a counseling relationship with someone is to say, "I am with you in what you are going through. Just as God is for you and your flourishing, I, too, am for you. With God's help, we will find a way forward together."

Understanding that God made us in his image helps us with this idea. God in three persons is in relationship with himself. And the Trinitarian God made us to be in relationship with him and one another. Jesus's great commandments—love your God and love your neighbor—are a logical outflowing of these realities. Relationships are preeminent in our God's personal experience, preeminent in his mind and heart. He intends his relationships to be united and influential. He intends our relationships to be united and influential.

Here again, our ability to form, build, and sustain an influential relationship with our counselees will be tied to how well we empathize and identify with their situation. Are we moved with compassion for what they are facing? Do we demonstrate curiosity, deference, and appreciation for the unique contexts they live within? Do we love, respond, and care for them in such a way that echoes the God who is for them? This is an opportunity to image God by being *for* our counselees. It's providing the sense and experience of "I am with you," a reflection of Jesus, who is God-with-us. Jesus, who is our peace in the midst of our struggles. Jesus, who is our ally. Jesus, who is our friend. These are the ways Jesus relates to us. And counselors can pattern after Jesus in how we relate to our counselees.

Indeed, to form good relationships, we must look to our God, to what is he like. This makes *our* personal relationship with the Lord so important, because when we know him well, then we represent him well. As we do life with the Lord, as we press in to knowing him more deeply, as we worship him with growing love and awe, as we mature in trusting him in ways that are increasingly becoming instinctive to our new nature, then we learn more intimately, in a firsthand way, what he is like. We receive from him; we are comforted by him. And that comfort becomes what we can offer to others (2 Corinthians 1:4–5). We give away what we have received from him.

As we depend on Jesus, he makes us righteous and "one who is righteous is a guide to his neighbor" (Proverbs 12:26). This proverb gives us yet another way to think about our work as biblical counselors: we aim to be a *guide* for counselees, who are, indeed, our neighbors. Because of our relationship with God, we serve as a humble guide in the paths and ways of the Lord.

CONCLUSION

To summarize, the focus of the beginning of the counseling process should be to build strong, trusting relationships with our counselees. As we embody Jesus's attributes and bear the fruit of the Holy Spirit, we contribute positively to establishing a relational dynamic in which our counselees can be helped. Empathy builds trust. Trust builds the relationship. People will only let a counselor guide them if they trust that the counselor cares about them. And the solidified relationship creates a context in which counseling can be one means for God to grow his people in godliness. Biblical counseling can be a means for a counselee to flourish—and to truly flourish is to grow up in every way into Christ (Ephesians 4:15).

The next chapter provides a flexible structure for how you can begin building that relationship during the very first session.

Chapter 3

THE FIRST SESSION

We know God has made people beautifully and wonderfully different. We also know that, because of the curse of sin, people struggle with problems that are vast and wide. Therefore, there is no one-size-fits-all approach to counseling. Similarly, no single approach always applies the first time you sit down with someone to offer help. Even so, there are ways you can be ready to conduct a first session so that it proves to be a productive time. What are those ways? How can you best ensure that a person leaving that first meeting with you feels hopeful about the help that can come from a fruitful counseling relationship?

To explore questions like these, this chapter is very detailed because of the importance of the first session in establishing rapport and providing people with an initial positive experience of counseling. But again, this book is not a how-to guide or a step-by-step manual. The components I will discuss will not all be present in every first counseling session. Variations occur for many reasons. Who is the individual in front of you? Why has this person come to counseling? How much time do you have to meet? Where does the conversation naturally go? The answers to each of these questions can impact the direction of a first session.

Before we explore how a first session might unfold, let's first think about the mindset we want to have as counselors as we begin a new relationship with a counselee.

THE COUNSELOR'S MINDSET

It's easy to think that a counselor isn't responsible for doing much in a first session. After all, you don't know this person yet, and you have a lot of listening to do. Isn't the first meeting the one time you can sit back and just get to know another person? Well, there is certainly a lot of listening ahead, but we will be more effective and loving helpers if we approach a first session with intentionality. What we do (or don't do) affects the future of this counseling relationship that is just coming into existence. I want all that I do and say as a counselor to be rooted in this reality: God intends for me (and for you!) to embody who he is, especially in living out the call to love one another well and wisely. My awareness of the following realities helps me to do that faithfully.

Something hurts. People don't come to counseling to talk about things that are going well. Something isn't working. Something is hard. If I hold in mind that something hurts, then my fundamental posture toward this person will be one of compassion (Colossians 3:12).

Pursuing counseling is not fun or easy. Who wants to go to counseling? Not many of us. Who wants to divulge sensitive and private information to someone we may have just met? Again, not many of us. If you have ever pursued counseling for yourself, you know that it is not an easy endeavor. Pursuing growth is difficult. You must be willing to admit that you have problems, and it requires humility to open up to someone and ask for help. You must be willing to hear and receive feedback, which requires the humility of listening. You must be willing to consider that feedback and implement changes in your life—how you think, act and react—which requires commitment and faith. You must be willing to put in time, effort, and maybe money, which requires sacrifice. It is no small thing when someone decides to pursue counseling, works out the scheduling details, and finally sits down to meet for the first time.

I try to put myself in the other person's shoes. As I remember that this person has made a choice to do something that I know is not easy, then I will look for ways to honor that choice by doing all I can to make the time helpful for the counselee (1 Thessalonians 5:11).

I do not yet know this person. I want to know this person. This is an individual with unique experiences. I have never heard this particular story. I want to build reasons for trust. Therefore, I go in humbly and ready to give my full attention. I am earnest to understand, earnest to listen, earnest to connect (Proverbs 18:4; Romans 12:9a).

Likewise, this person does not yet know me. I want this person to begin to know me. I want to be myself. I want the person to experience me as I always am, no matter what context I am in.

I want the counsel seeker to leave feeling hopeful and encouraged because something truly good has begun. Obviously a first session does not afford the time to comprehensively address problems. However, a good first session should leave the person feeling hopeful and encouraged that he or she can be helped and that counseling may be one effective way to bring about change and growth (Proverbs 15:22). This is a reasonable goal for a first session. Therefore, I will be on the lookout for ways to bring hope and encouragement throughout the conversation. I will likely offer specific and explicit encouragement toward the end of the session. I'll share an example of that later in the chapter.

HOW TO STRUCTURE A FIRST SESSION

In this section, I will present one way a first session could chronologically unfold. Here is an outline of this hypothetical first session:

- Review paperwork.
- Draw out and hear the person's story.
- Learn about the person's past counseling experiences.
- Identify the person's goals for counseling.
- Make a plan for the second session.
- Offer encouragement.
- Invite the person to ask any final questions.
- Close with prayer.

Let's look more deeply at each of these.

REVIEW THE PAPERWORK

After greeting the counselee and introducing myself, I raise the issue of the paperwork first. In a professional setting, the counselee will have read and signed a number of forms prior to the start of the first session. These forms generally contain important legal information about privacy rights as well as information about the counseling center's policies. It is important that the counselee understands this information. You are caring well for this person by ensuring that they understand these documents. So I offer an opportunity for the person to ask questions: "Do you have any questions about anything you read in the paperwork?"

If there are no questions, I review what kinds of situations warrant the breaking of counselor confidentiality. This includes, for example, the need to report child abuse to the proper governing authorities. Since people tend to skim over forms, be sure to highlight whatever you want the counselee to be aware of. You may wish to go over details like the cancellation policy or how the person can get in contact with you between sessions if a need arises. It can also be helpful for you to explicitly share the length of time of each counseling session so that it does not come as a surprise when you later transition to closing the session.

This is also a good time to make clear that you are a Christian who counsels from a Christian perspective. Since I work at a counseling center that has "Christian" in its name and our paperwork also discusses our approach as biblical counselors, I don't bring this up. If that is not as obvious for counselees who seek your help, then you can communicate that you are a biblical counselor and what that entails.

It is tempting to skip reviewing such matters because you really want to start getting to know this person, but let me encourage you not to skip this conversation. It is a way to love the person. If the counselee has clarity about the logistical and practical matters of counseling, then it can prevent future misunderstandings and frustrations for both of you.

DRAW OUT AND HEAR THE PERSON'S STORY

This is where the bulk of the time in a first session is usually spent. And it is here that you have the most opportunity to form a meaningful connection with the counselee. This connection lays a solid foundation for your relationship. It gives the person good reasons to come back and meet with you again.

Once the logistical parts of the paperwork have been discussed, the first major turning point in the conversation takes place. You move toward talking about deeper matters. Oftentimes, the paperwork also includes a form that gathers personal information and asks meaningful, deep questions. If so, discussing the person's responses to this form may be where you need to start. If not, start by asking a question or making a statement that invites the person to begin sharing their story. For example, "Can you share with me why you have decided to pursue counseling? And if it's okay, I might ask you some questions as you are talking, as well as take a few notes." (The second sentence helps the person know what to expect from me as they begin to talk.)

As you "hear the person's story," be an engaged listener. You are seeking to know another human being. You will learn details about this person's life, about their struggles, hopes, and disappointments. You will learn about the person's relationship with the Lord and where their understanding of God fits in relationship to the struggles. Getting to know someone is not done in an impersonal or passive way! So how can you be personal and engaging as the person shares their reasons for pursuing a counseling relationship? I will list six priorities that will demonstrate that you are seeking to understand and to care well. Many of these priorities are active listening skills, which are important to any session—whether it's the first or the thirtieth—so be sure to extend your use of them beyond the beginning of the process.

1. Periodically offer reflections and summaries. You want to be sure that you are accurately hearing what is being shared with you. So periodically check in by summarizing what you are hearing. This gives the counselee the opportunity to correct, clarify, or confirm your understanding of what has been shared. Your counselee is reading you, too, to see if you are tuned in to what is being said. Here is an example of a counselee sharing and a counselor summarizing and offering a reflection:

Counselee: Lately I have just felt like I'm drifting through life, and I'm not sure what my purpose is. I used to have so much motivation and so many clear goals for my life. But ever since I was let go from the job that I loved, I feel like every day is just a battle to feel normal. And even though God has blessed me and provided for me, I just haven't gotten back to that place where I feel the hope I once had. I want to feel the way that I used to. I miss approaching life with joy and optimism.

Counselor: You lost a job you loved, and you feel directionless and adrift?

Counselee: Yes, it was a devastating loss.

Counselor: I'm sorry that this has been so hard. It makes me really sad to hear how much pain this has caused you. (Silence) And since then, you've seen changes in yourself . . . and it's bothering you. The spark is gone. You want to regain the approach to life that you once had? And you want help because you're not sure how to do that?

Notice that I used some of the counselee's same words, but by primarily putting my understanding of the counselee's situation in my own words, I have given the counselee the opportunity to see if I accurately understand them. A summary captures content (loss of job and optimism), the person's emotion (discouragement, listlessness), and the direction the person wants to go (regain joy and optimism). A summary could also end with a question that furthers your understanding of the person and their struggles. In the above example, I could have ended my summary by asking, "How have you tried to deal with this sense of drifting?"

When these skills are used well, the conversation sounds vivid, not canned. If you are listening with attention, if you are listening to understand, if you are reaching to understand better, then your summary goes a little deeper and elaborates on what has been put on the table thus far. A good summary will generate real confidence in the counselee and a sense that the counselor "gets me." A good summary invites the person to open up to you further.

Notice that the personal reflection I shared—"I'm sorry that this has been so hard. It makes me really sad to hear how much pain this has caused you"—put me into the struggle. Share the ways you are moved by a person's story. Openhearted kindness and concern for another's troubles are characteristics of Jesus.

2. *Begin to understand the person's goals by clarifying how the person wants to use future counseling sessions.* Often as a person shares their immediate reasons for pursuing counseling, surrounding and peripheral issues will come up. If they do, you will need to check in to see if the counselee would like to explore these. For example, if a woman has come to address issues of intimacy in her marriage, and she mentions how she sometimes wonders what impact her parents' divorce has had on her own marriage, I might ask, "Is that something you'd like to explore during our times together?" In asking this, I am seeking to understand how our counseling sessions can be most helpful to her. It is natural to be curious and to ask about things that seem important to me, but I want to know what she views as important and relevant to the growth that she desires. I will take note of these clarifications so that I can bring them up later when we move to a more focused discussion of counseling goals.

3. *Freely express nonverbal communication to demonstrate that you are listening and engaged.* Look at the person. Make eye contact. Nod. Make "mm-hmm" sounds. Let your face match what you are hearing. Let genuine concern or grief or a twinkle of

humor be evident in your tone of voice. Remember, people are helped by real, personal relationships.

4. Listen for and process the emotions that are coming up in the moment. This is something you can do at any point in the session, depending on what you see in the counselee. Initiate a conversation about any emotions that you observe. For instance, many people are nervous in a first counseling session. If you notice this, then ask about it. For example, "You seem like you might be a little nervous right now. How are you doing?" If the person indeed feels nervous or awkward, then you have the opportunity to talk through and normalize those feelings. "I know it can feel strange to come in and talk about hard things with someone you just met. That's a really understandable feeling to have. Is there anything that I can do to help you feel more at ease?" This offer may result in a conversation about "lighter" matters.

If this is the case, keep in mind that although these kinds of conversations may not seem like the best use of the limited time available in a counseling session, they can help establish your relationship with your counselee. Recognizing what a person is ready for is an important aspect of learning how to walk alongside someone. People are ready to delve into issues and do the work of counseling at different paces. Part of your job is to stay in step with the person so you do not overwhelm them by going too quickly, or frustrate them by going too slowly. Tuning in to what this person is experiencing and feeling in the moment helps you to stay in step.

5. Listen for the person's interpretations and the implications of those interpretations. You are listening for how the person interprets circumstances, God, and themselves. Often interpretations that are false, misguided, or unbiblical contribute to the person's experience of the presenting problem. Therefore, counseling involves the work of helping the person think and interpret biblically, which we will explore in-depth in part 2 of this book. And although the bulk of this work will primarily take place in the middle of the counseling process, it starts with your first meeting. This is your first opportunity to begin to make sense of the person's world and understand how they are processing what is happening, what it means, and how it impacts their life and choices.

For example, perhaps the woman you are talking to seems nervous, and you have verbalized this to her. Because you have shared your observation, she goes on to explain her nervousness: "It is so scary for me to come and talk about my issues. When I am struggling, I feel like I am letting God down because I am not having the faith and hope that he says I should have." So, simply put, one of her interpretations is that when she is struggling, she is failing as a Christian. There are likely other interpretations, but this insight alone could be an early turning point.

Listen, too, for the implications of what is being said. Imagine if this same woman went on to say, "Because I feel like I am letting God down, I am ashamed to tell others about this struggle. If I do, then they will see how weak a Christian I really am." So, one implication of her interpretation is that she doesn't speak openly to others for fear of being exposed as the weak Christian she sees herself to be. This, too, is something that is worth coming back to in a future discussion. In a first session, though, let her keep talking while you keep listening to grow your understanding.

As you hear more about the contours of your counselee's struggles, listen for both interpretations and implications because they offer you potential entryways to address their struggles with biblical comfort and relief.

6. Explore potentially serious matters. Some people may be in a crisis situation when they arrive at a first session. You need to be prepared to respond appropriately to what is happening. Perhaps you are already aware that someone is in crisis because of the information shared in the intake process or when you first made arrangements to meet. Or something may come out in the course of the first session that gives you good reason to ask some searching questions and get a sense of what is going on.

For example, if you have learned that someone has a history of depression, then ask, "Have you ever struggled with suicidal thoughts?" If suicide or self-harm is a current struggle or has been in the past, do ask about their history of past struggles and attempts at self-harm. Assess how this person is doing today, and take immediate action if necessary. Talking plainly about suicide communicates that they can speak openly and frankly in the counseling session about what is going on in their heart. If self-destructive behavior is an issue, then you will need to follow up regularly. Talking about it early on and letting people know that you will regularly follow up on matters related to their safety sets a precedent for future conversations. Additional help on suicide assessment can be found in the resources section at the end of this book.

Similarly, you need to be prepared to ask further questions about abuse if you suspect or know that something abusive has happened. Sexual violation? Physical violence? Verbal aggression? Is your counselee currently in danger? Get enough details to know what happened, when it happened, and with whom. This kind of knowledge is crucial for you to have, and, here again, you may need to take immediate action. At the very least, it helps you consider how to best care for the person and to identify starting points for deeper conversations. See also the resources section for direction on matters of abuse.

LEARN ABOUT THE PERSON'S PAST COUNSELING EXPERIENCES

After getting a good sense of the reasons the person is pursuing counseling, it is helpful to know if they have had counseling in the past for this issue. If yes, ask what was helpful or unhelpful about those past counseling experiences. This information can help guide what directions to explore.

This inquiry dovetails into the larger matter of what "voices" are in the person's life. Who—for good or for ill—is speaking or has spoken into the person's situation? Is there a pastor or church involved? Is a spouse supportive and willing to be involved in the counseling process in any way? What books, websites, and friends play a significant role?

IDENTIFY THE PERSON'S GOALS FOR COUNSELING

Next, the conversation can transition to the person's goals for counseling. One or more goals may have already emerged naturally as the person told their story and explained their reason for pursuing counseling. You can use any of that information to transition to naming goals. You may say, "It sounds like you'd like to grow in your understanding of what biblical forgiveness looks like and how it plays out in the relationships where you see that you have become bitter. Are there any other goals you have in mind for our times together?"

Identifying goals is often an exercise in collaboration. Those who come for counsel might feel stuck and unable to identify solutions. They might need help framing the goals biblically because they are not even sure what they should aim for. Additionally, you can summarize to help concisely capture what you are hearing about how the person wants to grow. Some people may need time to think through their goals more deeply, so setting goals does not need to be confined to the first session. You can follow up in the next session if goals are unclear after this initial conversation.

Discussing goals is important because it clarifies what the counselee and the counselor will be working on together. This conversation can also shed light on what role the counselee wants the counselor to play. I always write goals down because they will need to be revisited periodically in the future. We will need to assess together where the counselee is in the counseling process, how we are doing in our times in relation to accomplishing these goals, and whether we have veered off track and need a course correction. And oftentimes goals will change and develop as our understanding of the problems becomes clearer through the counseling process. So goals at this point might be a list of what the person wants to address in counseling, rather than a list of desired outcomes. We will revisit goals in chapter 8.

MAKE A PLAN FOR THE SECOND SESSION

After the person has shared with me some goals, I ask the counselee to prioritize the list of goals. Once I learn what the counselee sees as most important to explore first, then I ask a simple question like, "Well, how about we start there next time?" If the counselee agrees, then we have a short-term plan. It can feel hopeful for the counselee to know where the next session is heading. We're already making progress. Further, having a plan that has been agreed upon by both of us increases the likelihood that the person will come back.

Near the end of the session, I also ask the person to be thinking about other parts of their story that would be important to share with me in our second session.

OFFER ENCOURAGEMENT

Tell this person that you are encouraged by their step of faith in coming for counseling. As I mentioned earlier, it is no small feat for someone to come and ask for help. As biblical counselors, we want to have eyes that see this decision has taken courage and faith. When we recognize this as an act of faith, we then want to speak those good words so that our counselee can be encouraged too. It takes the work of the Spirit of God to come humbly for help, and we don't want to miss the opportunity to point out the Spirit's activity in this person's life.

Remember the woman I mentioned earlier who was feeling nervous during our time together? With her, I would specifically share that I am encouraged that she spoke with me about her problem because it is hard for her to let people know when she is hurting. By telling me about it, she is already moving in the right direction. This may seem small, but it is a significant step of faith. I want to point it out as a step of faith so that she can be encouraged to see how God is already at work and to know that his work in her is recognizable to me.

If I have enough information about her specific struggle and can make a connection to the Bible, then I might also offer a verse or passage to encourage her. I might turn to Psalm 34:5 and briefly speak about God's pleasure when we turn to him in faith. As we look to the Lord in faith and in expectation of his help, as this woman is doing, then we are "radiant." Reading about God in this light can begin to reshape what she believes God thinks about her. Her beliefs can also be reshaped by how I react to her disclosures, so my attitude toward what she feels is "shameful and weak" must mirror God's attitude.

INVITE THE PERSON TO ASK ANY FINAL QUESTIONS

I like to check in once more before we conclude. I am interested in answering any questions the counseling experience has raised. I find people often do have at least one question. For example, people often want to know how long a season of counseling tends to last. If so, I use it as an opportunity to agree on a schedule. I might say, "How about we meet weekly for four weeks and then reevaluate after that? Depending on our progress, we can continue to meet weekly or perhaps switch to biweekly meetings at that point."

CLOSE WITH PRAYER

Finally, ask if you can close the time in prayer. Consider mentioning the reasons the person has come to counseling and connecting their needs to a specific aspect of the Lord's care. I also commit our future counseling sessions to the Lord and ask him to bless and work through them.

As you can see, this hypothetical example of a first session covers a lot of ground. You may not be able to get through all of these matters in the first session. If the counselee is very upset, you might barely get through any of it! That's ok. Your counselee is a person—not a project. Your aim is to begin to know this person truly, not get through a first session to-do list. Nothing is as important as seeking to know, love, and respond appropriately to the person in front of you.

BE INTENTIONAL

As you read this outline of a first session, perhaps you have been evaluating your own first session practices and methods. Here are a few questions to help you process what we have covered:

- What do you make sure to cover in a first session?

- Have you identified any strengths and weaknesses in your approach?
- Are you considering any adjustments for your ministry setting?

Though there is no formula or one right way to organize a first counseling session, you want to be intentional with what you are doing. You will be more likely to accomplish good with and for another person if you know what you're aiming for and have reasons for doing what you choose to do.

To summarize, our aims in a first session are to welcome the troubled, provide safety, cultivate trust, and give hope.

AFTER THE FIRST SESSION

Following a first session, you should take notes. Counselors where I work are required to keep a note in a person's file for each session, but I advise doing so even if you don't have to! I say this because I know my own memory can easily fail me, and my notes are useful as I prepare for upcoming sessions. Reviewing notes is also a way to honor the investment the person is making by coming to counseling. People feel cared for as they see you have remembered details of what they shared with you. Remembering is a way to build trust because people see you stewarding what they previously shared with you.

Time between sessions allows you to research, read up on subjects that pertain to what the counselee is seeking help for, or consult with a colleague who has experience with this situation. Doing so is especially important when you do not have as much experience with a particular problem.

For example, if I'm counseling someone who is preparing to marry a divorcee with children and I have yet to counsel someone in that particular situation, I can prepare for this case by seeking out resources that come from the vantage point of my counselee. What's it like to forge a relationship with adolescents as a stepparent? What's it like to form a relationship with your new spouse's ex as you take on a parental role with their children? What are typical challenges of this familial dynamic?

Seeking out resources are not replacements for doing the work of getting to know this individual, but it will help you start to imagine what it is like to be in this person's shoes. And sometimes when people are walking through uncharted territory themselves, they need help putting their experience into words. Your sense of what the experience might be like can serve them well as you find the words together.

Chapter 4

THE SECOND SESSION

The second session is worth exploring in some depth because of its unique position as a transition point from the first session to the rest of the counseling process.

HOW TO STRUCTURE A SECOND SESSION

The second session tends to be less structured than the first session. However, I have found the following structure to be a fruitful way to organize my time with my counselees during the second session. The outline below assumes that the first session outline was completed. If it wasn't, then you will be sure to cover those aspects of the first session that have yet to be addressed.

- Set expectations for how sessions tend to begin moving forward.
- Ask for reflections about the first session.
- Learn more about the person's story.
- Begin working on the person's top priority.

Let's discuss each of these.

SET EXPECTATIONS FOR HOW SESSIONS TEND TO BEGIN MOVING FORWARD

After greetings, I share with counselees what they can expect at the beginning of our sessions moving forward. To do this, I say something along these lines: "Since this is our second meeting, I want to share how I will usually start our times together. I will ask about the time between this session and our last to check in with you to see whether something has happened since our last session that you would like to talk about in our time together today. If there isn't, then we can pick up where we left off in our last conversation and jump right in with what we had planned to talk about. But I always want to leave room for you to take us in another direction if something is on your heart and will be helpful to you."

Explicit comments like this help set expectations, which people appreciate. A counseling relationship is different than the usual way people get to know each other. It's a relationship with more structure, focus, and time limitations, and communicating about the process helps maximize the time you have.

ASK FOR REFLECTIONS ABOUT THE FIRST SESSION

Because a lot happened in the first session and because time has passed since the first session, you can provide an opportunity for the person to share any reflections or questions they have had since your initial meeting. Here are some open-ended questions you can ask that fit well in a second session: How did you experience the first session? Did anything stand out? Is there anything we should circle back to right away?

LEARN MORE ABOUT THE PERSON'S STORY

In a second session, I am ready to learn more about the person's story. I can draw this out by following up on what I asked them to be thinking about at the end of our first session: What else is important for me to know early on as I come alongside you to offer help? This question provides an effective way to hear more details of the person's story that are germane to the reason that the individual is seeking help.

At this point, the details of what the person shares aren't all necessarily connected. That's okay, and there is no pressure for you, as the counselor, to start making connections. You are getting to know this person, and you want to hear what seems important to them. You can't and won't know what it all means yet, but you are learning what is meaningful to the counselee, and that's worthwhile!

As you continue to listen actively while your counselee shares more, perhaps they will have already talked about their life of faith. If not, now could be a good time to invite them to share: "Tell me about your faith." After interacting about what the counselee shares with you, a natural follow-up would be to ask how they see their faith intersecting with the issues that have brought them to counseling. Has their faith afforded them certain helps and comforts in the midst of trouble? Are they learning to lean on God in a way they never have before? What is their sense of God's direction for the situation they're in? These kinds of questions will dovetail nicely, too, with the larger discussion of goals. That is, most counselees seeking biblical counseling will want the Lord and their faith to factor into the outcomes they hope to see through counseling.

BEGIN WORKING ON THE PERSON'S TOP PRIORITY

In this session, you can also start to go deeper in the area that the counselee identified as a top priority in the first session. As you begin to explore a struggle more deeply, realize that talking about the problem might be painful for the person. But as you invite them to keep speaking about what hurts, you validate that what is happening in his or her life *matters*. It matters to the person. It matters to God. It matters to you.

If the person is pursuing counseling in order to address an area of personal sin and moral failure, then they might feel ashamed to be exposed before you. Remember, you are an ambassador. You represent Christ in how you hear and respond to the details of this person's story. Christ came for the sick, and he knew what he was getting into when he came for us. Sin doesn't surprise him or catch him off guard. He is not too disgusted by sin to hear disgusting details. And even as Christ wants our repentance, at the same time he has realistic expectations for the messiness of how repentance gets worked out. He is patient. Through love, he perseveres on the road of repentance with hope.

Represent Christ in how you hear and respond to the realities that this person would rather leave in the dark but is instead bringing into the light. Embody Christ and the truth that he is not afraid to draw near to this person. We can bring ourselves to God as we are, even if we are messy, and even if we are struggling with God himself. We can bring our questions to him. It is safe to struggle in his presence. Make it safe for this person to struggle in your presence. Take this image from Psalm 40:1 and embody it: "he [God] inclined to me and heard my cry." We believe and trust God is inclined to listen to this person's story. He leans in. He takes in every word. He is invested in this person, and he cares so much. How can you reflect this in the counseling room?

CONCLUSION

In a second session, the same overarching principles discussed in the previous chapter apply. Encourage people to speak freely about what is happening in their lives. Listen and respond in ways that embody Jesus. Be attentive, and be moved by what you hear. Remember that you are in the presence of one of God's beloved children. You are called to reflect the Father's heart in how you listen and respond; your presence and your words should reflect to your counselee his compassion, his mercy, and his tenderness toward shame.

Chapter 5

A CASE STUDY IN THE BEGINNING: NADIA

Nadia[1] is a thirty-two-year-old single, African-American woman. In the past two years, she finished her medical residency and obtained her first job as a surgeon in a large hospital located in the center of a city. Because of the hospital's location, many patients come in with life-threatening, critical injuries. On her intake forms, Nadia disclosed that she is seeking counseling because she has been "experiencing panic at work."

THE FIRST SESSION WITH NADIA

In this section I will fill in the outline from chapter 3 with details from my first session with Nadia.

DISCUSS PRELIMINARIES

I shared privacy policies and gave Nadia an opportunity to ask me questions. She did not have any questions about the

---

1. I changed Nadia's identifying details, and the process I describe with her is a composite from several of my counseling cases over the years.

counseling forms and explained that, as a doctor, she was aware of her privacy rights.

DRAW OUT AND HEAR THE PERSON'S STORY

I opened up this part of the conversation by letting Nadia know I had read in her intake forms that she is seeking counseling because of feeling panic at work. Then I asked her to tell me more about what had been happening. As she talked, I asked Nadia several questions to get a better sense of what was currently happening. Imagine the following questions over the course of a thirty-minute conversation, not one right after the other:

- "Are there certain situations at work when the feeling of panic comes on?"
- "When you describe yourself as 'panicked,' what does that feel like? Do you feel panic in your body? Where?"
- "What kinds of thoughts are you having when you feel the panic?"
- "What do you do when you feel panic at work?"
- "Do the things you do in response bring relief?"

A little later in the conversation, I gently shared why I asked such pointed questions: "I really want to understand what this experience of panic is like for you." Questions like these did help me gain an accurate sense of Nadia's experience. "Panic" can look and feel different to different people, so I didn't want to assume that I knew what it was like for Nadia.

LEARN ABOUT THE PERSON'S PAST COUNSELING EXPERIENCES

I asked Nadia if this was her first experience in counseling. Since she confirmed that it was her first, I asked her if she had any questions about the counseling process. She told me that she was not sure what to expect from counseling, but she didn't have any questions. I asked her how she found out about my counseling center, and she told me that someone from her church had mentioned it to her. I then asked her a couple questions to hear about her involvement at church.

IDENTIFY THE PERSON'S GOALS FOR COUNSELING

Nadia had a clear sense of why she was pursuing counseling. She was troubled by her panic at work and wanted help with managing it. I did ask if she had any other areas of life that she wanted to discuss during our times together, and she answered none that she could think of.

MAKE A PLAN FOR THE NEXT SESSION

Since Nadia was clear about her goal for counseling, I wanted to use the time between sessions to build momentum. I asked her to keep track of her panic episodes between now and our next session. If she experienced panic before our next session, I asked her to pay attention to these kinds of things: What happened right before you started to feel panic? Where are you feeling the panic in your body? What are your thoughts? What do you do in response to what you're feeling and thinking?

I wanted to gain details from Nadia's answers to these questions because I was still learning about the contours of her experience. My intention was that this "assignment" would also help raise her own self-awareness of the panic experiences and possibly provide insights that would prove helpful to our counseling process.

This type of assignment between the first and second session can be used for many presenting problems and is an effective way to learn about the nature and shape of the problem. For example, if a spouse comes in alone because of increased conflict in a marital relationship, then you could ask the person to keep track of conflicts between sessions: What precipitated the conflict? How did you respond to your spouse? How did you feel during the conflict? After it? Did you reconcile? How?

After Nadia agreed to think through these questions when she had another panic episode, I told her that we would begin our conversation with these questions next time, along with her sharing anything else she thinks might be helpful for me to know as I start to walk with her. Nadia agreed that this was a good plan for our next meeting.

OFFER ENCOURAGEMENT

I told Nadia that I admired her for reaching out for help. She saw that the problem was getting worse, and she showed intentionality in locating a resource to address it. That takes courage, I told her, and I thanked her for what she had shared with me.

INVITE THE PERSON TO ASK ANY FINAL QUESTIONS

As I offered her a last chance to ask questions, Nadia asked me if I wanted to be in touch with her pastor, mentioning that the intake form had asked for her pastor's name. I told her that I'd be happy to do so with her permission. I explained that it has been fruitful in my experience to be able to share with pastors what their congregants are working on in counseling so that the pastor, and maybe others in the church body, could pray and follow up with her. Nadia expressed both a curiosity about and openness toward this kind of coordination, so we agreed to revisit the conversation soon.

CLOSE IN PRAYER

This was my prayer at the end of the session: "Lord, what a pleasure to meet Nadia today. I am thankful for how she was brave to seek help for these hard feelings of panic. I thank you that you know and understand and care about this panic she has been experiencing. As she and I get to know each other, Lord, please help me understand it too. We commit this season of counseling to you and ask that you use it as a way to relieve Nadia's anxiety. In Jesus's name, amen."

AFTER THE FIRST SESSION

After the first session, I thought and brainstormed about what would be helpful for me to know based on Nadia's counseling goal. I considered the following:

- What is her overall work environment like?
- How would she describe her colleagues?
- How would she describe the hospital's ethos?
- What drew Nadia to this particular job, which seems intense even for a hospital?
- What drew her to medical school in the first place?
- Had she always wanted to be a surgeon, and what about being a surgeon suits her?
- What is it like to be a woman in a field with a male majority, and what is it like to be a Black woman in this field?
- I did learn that Nadia attends church, but what more can I learn about her faith and church involvement?
- How does Nadia's faith come to bear on the panic she is experiencing? How does she imagine God views her in the midst of panic? To what degree might she find her faith relevant to addressing panic?
- I'm aware of the cultural and ethnic differences between Nadia and me. Might there be aspects of her panic experiences at work that are influenced by her cultural and

ethnic identity that I need to understand? I am putting this on my radar as something to follow up on.

Understanding matters like these might not prove to be essential to what will help Nadia with her presenting problem of panic in the workplace. But they also might turn out to yield helpful insights, and the beginning of counseling is a time to explore many angles because I'm not sure yet what is most important.

THE SECOND SESSION WITH NADIA

This section will follow the same pattern as the section on Nadia's first session. I will flesh out the outline with details of my second session with Nadia.

SET EXPECTATIONS FOR HOW SESSIONS TEND TO BEGIN MOVING FORWARD

In the second session, I let Nadia know that in this and our subsequent sessions I will always be glad to diverge from our plan if something has happened that would be helpful to talk about for today's session. She did not opt for this today, and so I asked her if she had thought of anything else that would be helpful for me to know as I begin to walk alongside her.

ASK FOR REFLECTIONS ABOUT THE FIRST SESSION

Nadia reflected that she had expected our first session to feel a bit like when she meets her patients for the first time, and that it would carry the feel of an interview. She was pleasantly surprised that our first session was more like a conversation than it was me acquiring data and information about her history. I laughed and told her I was glad for that!

LEARN MORE ABOUT THE PERSON'S STORY

Nadia said she thought I should know that her parents are Togolese immigrants and came to the United States before she was born. She said it had always been her parents' dream and intention for her and her sister to become doctors; this path was laid out for her at a young age. I asked her how she feels about this long-held dream of her parents, and we spent the majority of the session talking through this jumping-off point that she had put on the table.

This conversation provided a natural time for me to raise our racial and cultural differences and demonstrate my eagerness to understand that which I haven't personally experienced. "Your mention of your family's immigration reminds me that you and I come from different cultures and races, and I really want to understand your life from your perspective. If it's okay with you, I'd like to keep conversations about culture and race an open door for our times together, and be able to discuss those topics when or if your particular experiences might bear on something you're describing or wrestling with. How does that sound to you?" Nadia expressed her openness to this suggestion.

Let me make a comment on this: even if a natural avenue hadn't emerged, I would've raised this with Nadia because it is so important that we as counselors take care to acknowledge differences. It is so important that we demonstrate both curiosity and humility to understand life from a person's perspective. God created differences—they are his good idea—and we are people who are impacted by our differences. We are born embedded in particular bodily, social, cultural, racial, historical, and religious contexts, and any or all of these can be relevant to situations in a person's life. Knowing this, biblical counselors will be alert, sensitive to, and ready to talk about any of these features as the counselee desires, or as needed in order to understand the individual better.

Next, I asked Nadia about her faith. "I know you mentioned you belong to a church, and I'm wondering about your personal journey of faith. Can you share more with me?"

BEGIN WORKING ON THE PERSON'S TOP PRIORITY

Aware of the time we had remaining, I asked if she had had a panic experience at work between sessions. She said she did, and she pulled out a notebook to share with me what she had written about the experience. What she shared helped me better understand the kind of panic that is troubling her and had brought her to counseling. Given that Nadia works in a high-stress environment, I could imagine a thousand different scenarios that could be panic provoking, so it was informative to hear what specifically brought on the feeling for her. It also started to raise questions in my mind about what might be the problem under the problem. By this I mean that Nadia is aware of and able to express that she feels panicked. But what is fueling the panic? Her story of her most recent experience of panic enabled me to start hypothesizing. But I still needed to know more.

At the end of the second session, I asked her to do the same activity for our third session—to write down a few details if she had a panic-inducing event at work. I thanked her for what she had brought to our time today and encouraged her that her intentionality and follow-through would prove helpful for our times together. I closed the session in prayer.

AFTER THE SECOND SESSION

After this second session, what were my thoughts and observations? I was not sure yet why Nadia had brought up her parents' immigration to the United States. She had not made a direct connection between her parents' desire for her to become a doctor and her panic at work. Is there one? For now, I am content to write down and remember that she found these details about her family's story important to share with me. It could be that they are connected to her presenting problem but not necessarily. Nadia hadn't spoken about her parents as if their hopes for her career had bothered her; rather, she spoke of them and their desires for her in a matter-of-fact way. As we talked, I had primarily sensed that she felt proud of accomplishing what her parents had hoped for her. Out loud to her, I had surmised how proud her parents must be of her and expressed my respect for the hard work she had put in to become the surgeon she is today.

I was also thinking about where some of the differences in culture might be. In my cultural and ethnic background as a White American, I might view living up to a parent's desires as oppressive, as a limitation on my ability to explore my own interests. But Nadia didn't speak of it that way. I want to be careful to not speak about her parents' desires as if they might be a problem for her, when they might not be.

From her reflections about her faith, I was able to get a sense of her spiritual commitment and involvement. As she talked about her history with the Lord, I noticed she several times described him as "generous" to her. I wrote this word down to remember. Any time you hear someone using the same word repeatedly, key into it. It can reveal something especially important or meaningful to them. It might also be worth pointing out and getting a fuller sense of its meaning to the person as they reflect on what the word means to them. In this case, it might be a word I intentionally use later when I am speaking to Nadia about the Lord; it could be a way to frame something that is likely to resonate with her, given her use of the word and her personal experiences of God's character.

I'm also impressed that Nadia took seriously my request that she record details about her feelings of panic. This tells me she is motivated to make progress, and it also shows that she trusted my recommendation enough to do this as a step toward accomplishing her goal for counseling.

Chapter 6

CONSIDERATIONS AT THE BEGINNING

In this brief chapter, I will provide a list of questions to help you reflect on the beginning process of forming a new counseling relationship. These considerations might not work themselves out in actual conversations with the person, but they are intended to provide you with a chance to slow down and be thoughtful, reflective, and prayerful as you begin working with a new counselee. They are intended to help you grow in self-awareness, which is a characteristic that is important for a counselor to possess. You are bringing yourself to the counseling room with all of your presuppositions, lenses, biases, tendencies, and assumptions. We all have these, and it's natural and unavoidable, but the goal is to be aware of them so that we are better able to serve others.

The questions are in no particular order.

- *How are you experiencing this person so far?* Think about the person's observable emotions, body language, and word choices to help you put words to this.

- *What assumptions are you making about the person and/or the presenting problem?* One way to discern this is to examine any impulses to move in a specific direction based on what you've heard. You certainly can explore matters that seem important to you to "test" the accuracy and validity of your assumptions; the caution here is not to proceed as if your assumptions are true or your inclinations as to what the person needs are the right ones. Also, if you happen to share with your counselee the same or a similar issue, you might need to work harder to stay objective and not make assumptions about the person's experience.

- *What information seems most important to you so far, and what information seems most important to your counselee?* Even though you are just beginning to get to know this person, you are naturally thinking biblically about what is going on and how the Lord speaks to that. Think about how you're interpreting the counselee's situation so far as a way to lead you to identify what you might need to explore next with the person.

- *What does the person repeat?* This can give you clues about what is most important to the person.

- *Have any topics come up that feel out of your depth?* What are you going to do about it?

- *Are there cultural and/or racial differences between you and your counselee?* How can you demonstrate cultural humility?

- *What is it like for you to come into proximity with the kind of struggle this person is facing?* How does this kind of struggle make you feel?

- *Are you starting to get a fuller picture of the person's life?* Knowing your counselee's relationships, employment, church involvement, community involvement, physical health, relational support, and cultural background will help you see what the person might leverage and build upon to bring relief to the area that is hurting. Which of these might be helpful to find out about, based on what you have heard so far?

- *Have you noticed strengths in this person?* What are they, and how might you both access and build upon them in order to help the person with their counseling goals?

- *How is the person responding to you?* What is your sense of how the relationship between you and the counselee is growing?

- *How can you help the counselee use time in between sessions to build upon what you are working on together?* The hard work of growing and changing requires consistent investment, so we want the work we're doing in counseling to carry on in a counselee's everyday life. We can facilitate this by what is often referred to as "assigning homework." My general approach to this is to collaborate with the counselee near the end of a session to identify a natural, organic step to be working on in between sessions that builds momentum for what we are working on. For example, I asked Nadia to keep track of details about her panic experiences to then share with me in our next session. I will offer more examples in chapters moving forward, though I won't use the word "homework." I have also included an article on the subject in the Resources section.

THE END OF THE BEGINNING

We will not venture beyond the second session in part 1, though this does not mean that the tasks of the beginning are over after two sessions. The time period that constitutes the beginning, middle, and end will, of course, vary depending on the person, what they share and when, and which issues they are seeking to address. This is why I have identified the major tasks of each phase so that you have an overarching idea of the primary focus for each part of the process, however long each phase may be.

Here is a summary of the primary tasks of the beginning:

The first task is to seek to get to know the person and understand the matters that have brought them to counseling. Through your interactions with the person, and through your summaries and reflections about the matters on the person's heart, the counselee should be able to affirm by the end of the beginning that you have successfully grasped what they have shared with you. The person believes that you are well on the way to knowing them.

The second task is to build reasons for the person to trust you by how you have cared for them thus far. As Christ's ambassador in the counseling room, you must represent Christ's heart and concern, enabling your counselee to experience you as someone who deserves their trust. Because the person has started to feel known by you, and because you have earned their trust, you have now positioned yourself to steward the influence of your role in ways that will be meaningful and helpful in the person's life.

To consider these two tasks together, we could say that the desired outcome of the beginning of the counseling process is for the counselee to possess this kind of sentiment: *"My counselor understands the concerns on my heart, and I trust my counselor to journey forward with me as I seek God's mercies for the struggles that I face."*

In other words, you have built a trusted counseling relationship. If this is true for the counselee, we can be hopeful and expectant for how God will work in the middle of the process. We will turn there next.

Part 2:
The Middle of the
Counseling Process

The primary focus of the middle of the counseling process is helping your counselee learn how to see their situation through the lens of Scripture and how to act on those new insights. Thus, the two major tasks of the middle of the counseling process are to guide your counselee in:

1. Interpreting biblically the matters and concerns for which the counselee is seeking help, and
2. Imagining a faithful way forward by applying biblical wisdom and pursuing biblical priorities.

Chapter 7

INTERPRETING BIBLICALLY

*"Without You, what am I to myself but a guide
to my own self-destruction?"*—St. Augustine[1]

The end of chapter 2 offered another metaphor for our work as counselors: we serve as a guide. In stark words, St. Augustine's quote above reminds us why we need one. Without the right guide, we will lead ourselves only to death. Proverbs captures a similar idea: "There is a way that *seems* right to a man, but its end is the way to death" (Proverbs 14:12, emphasis added). Indeed, warnings abound in Scripture. Hosea 4:14 says, "People without understanding shall come to ruin." These are all sobering words. The way we are inclined to go "seems right." But it leads to self-destruction and ruin. It leads to death.

Thankfully, mercifully, Scripture gives us more than just warnings. Both Augustine and Proverbs 14:12 succinctly reveal our deepest need: we need someone outside ourselves to save us from ourselves. And of course, the "You" in Augustine's quote is Jesus. We will not find our way out of our trouble on our own. The way that seems right isn't right. We need someone

---

1. From *The Confessions of Saint Augustine.*

to come find us and put us on the Way. Thankfully, mercifully, God gave us Jesus to guide us on the way to life everlasting. Supremely, Jesus himself is the Way (John 14:6).

As his people, as those who Jesus has found, rescued, and put on the Way everlasting, we now, too, can guide people and help them keep on the path. I don't mean this in a salvific sense because of course only Jesus can put people on the Way. There may be times in counseling that God uses us to point to the Way for those who don't yet know Jesus as their Savior. But for our purposes, think of counselors as guiding by playing a role in helping people locate Jesus's way in the midst of their circumstances and struggles. We partner with people to seek and find understanding.

Why might someone need such help? Because we often lack wisdom. Our situation isn't always clear to us. The way forward gets hazy. *Where do I go from here? How do I make sense of what has happened? What does God call me to do now?* Sometimes the way forward is not even hazy; it's pitch black. *Where is God in this? Is there any hope if I can't see any way forward?* These may be the types of questions on people's hearts when they seek counseling. So as biblical counselors, we aim to be skillful and wise at identifying with people what a faithful way forward could look like for them in their particular set of circumstances. This brings us to one of the main tasks of the middle of the counseling process.

When the beginning of the process has successfully resulted in you, the counselor, accurately knowing the person and the person's situation, then you are able to make sense of what is happening. Working together, you and the counselee *interpret* the person's situation according to the Bible's wisdom, the wisdom that comes from above. Once you interpret the situation accurately, you and the counselee are ready to *imagine* a faithful way forward.

In this chapter and the next, we'll explore both. To capture these two tasks, I'll offer a counseling case that demonstrates what happens when we interpret wrongly and thus imagine wrongly. Then I will contrast it with what happens in that same case when we interpret rightly and thus imagine rightly.

INTERPRET

The Trinitarian God is the only one with the knowledge and objectivity required to see accurately. We need him to share his interpretations so that we are not lost. We need his Word to light our path so we know where we should go (Psalm 119:105). This also means we need to adopt his interpretive gaze so we can make sense of our lives and understand what is most important. And what is most important? Jesus's two great commandments loom large and ever present for us in our counseling work with people. We want to journey with people toward wise understanding of how they can love God with all their heart, soul, mind, and strength as well as love their neighbors as they love themselves.

What does that kind of love look like, and how can people faithfully pursue it, given their unique circumstances? To find answers to this question, we must first accurately assess what is happening. This brings us to the importance of the interpretive task. In the counseling profession, this task is often referred to as "conceptualization," but I prefer "interpretation" because it's a less technical word and less abstract. *Interpret* also has clearer links to the Bible—it's closely related to discernment—and reminds us more readily of what we seek to do as biblical counselors. To come to an accurate interpretation means that we have received from God a kind of guidance that leads to understanding. "Let my cry come before you, O Lord; *give me understanding* according to your word!" (Psalm 119:169, emphasis added). "Lord, give us understanding"… this is what we seek with our counselees. This is what we need to cry out for with our counselees as we search together for a faithful interpretation that accurately reflects and displays God's knowledge and wisdom that he has revealed in Scripture.

Here then begins the extended counseling example that will first demonstrate the significance of the interpretive task:

A married man, Andre, comes to individual counseling and tells his counselor he is so discouraged with his marriage. "My wife is an angry woman," Andre says. "She is unhappy with everything I do, and nothing pleases her. Worse than that, she makes her contempt known to me on an almost daily basis."

Now imagine Andre's counselor is a good listener but doesn't ask many questions. Andre seems so earnest, so distraught. The counselor feels compassion for him. He really seems like he is suffering (and he probably is). In the first weeks of counseling, Andre comes in with his most recent story of how he feels let down by his wife. He is becoming hopeless for his marriage. The counselor takes on a consoling role.[2] The counselor wants to alleviate Andre's suffering, and so he agrees with him that, yes, his wife's attitude toward him sounds so hard. The counselor expresses sorrow that Andre is living with and enduring an angry woman.

What is happening here? Andre came to counseling with this interpretation: "My wife is angry. I am a victim of her anger, and I have no responsibility in it." He didn't say his perspective in such stark terms, but this was the essence of it. The stories he shared about their interactions and the way he portrayed himself as an actor in those stories would lead any listener to conclude this was

2. Taking on a consoling role is one of several pitfalls when counseling a spouse about marital concerns in individual counseling. For more instruction on this counseling scenario, see Lauren Whitman and Aaron Sironi, "Marriage Counseling with Only One Spouse," *Journal of Biblical Counseling* 33, no. 2 (2019).

Andre's interpretation. The counselor's misstep is to hear Andre's interpretation of what is happening and agree with it, to accept the narrative as true according to how Andre tells it. As the counselor does this, Andre feels validated. Finally, someone gets him and sees how hard it is to be married to this kind of person.

Andre, and now the counselor, have both interpreted his problem wrongly. To understand how they got to this point, we have to go back to the tasks of the beginning of the counseling process. Instead of seeking to know Andre and his situation accurately, the counselor accepted what Andre said without getting a full picture of what was contributing to his experience of having an "angry wife." Andre is truly blind to himself in the ways that relate to what is happening in his wife's heart. All he knows is that she is angry; he doesn't know why, and he hasn't shown care or concern to understand why. A counselor can help him do this work, but it takes time. It takes a lot of time in this instance for the counselor to really know Andre's situation because the counselor doesn't know Andre's wife and can't ask her for her perspective. But to love Andre and to love his wife, the counselor must go slowly and, again, be careful not to jump on board with Andre's perspective.

Now let's change how the counselor responded to and engaged with Andre's presenting problem. Imagine that the counselor made a move like this in the beginning of the process, instead of agreeing with Andre's interpretation that his wife was angry and he was the victim in the relationship.

> **Counselor:** In our first sessions together, you've shared with me how hard it is to be in your marriage. Your wife is angry with you and, to some degree or another, she lets you know that almost daily. You live on heightened alert to her anger, and you've helped me understand

how painful this is for you. That grieves me. As we've been talking, I can't help but think about anger and the nature of it. We know anger is usually connected to something, sometimes many things, right? [Andre nods.] Do you feel like you know what those things might be for your wife?

Before we explore how Andre responds, I'd like to highlight how the counselor's engagement with Andre in this example demonstrates the empathy described in chapter 2. Remember that empathy is not agreement with someone's interpretation. The counselor's statement here shows that the counselor has worked hard to understand Andre's experience of his marriage and feels pain for the ways that Andre is suffering. That is empathy. The counselor is moved by Andre's experience. Regardless of why their marriage is suffering, it is suffering. Andre and his wife are not enjoying the blessing of a united, connected marriage, and for that we can rightfully express our sadness to Andre. From that point of compassion and understanding, empathy now says, "I care so much about how you're suffering that I want to help you in ways that are truly helpful." As we're starting to see from this example, Andre won't be helped in lasting ways if the counselor naively agrees with his interpretation. That would not be empathy. That would not be biblical love.

Returning to Andre's counseling session, it becomes clear that he isn't sure why his wife is angry. He lists a number of small concerns that his wife has voiced, such as his forgetfulness in clearing his plate from the table after dinner. The counselor continues to probe here: "I could see how that would be irritating if she feels like she has to clean up after you. Hmm... But it doesn't seem to add up that she could be as angry as you describe for something like that, does it? I'm wondering if there is more there for her. What do you think?" Andre can't come up with anything.

This leads to a natural next step for the unfolding counseling process. They decide that Andre will initiate a conversation with his wife in a calm moment. He will tell her that he strongly senses she is angry with him, very angry, but that he has recently realized he doesn't know why. As basic as this sounds, it is a light-bulb moment for him: *She's angry. I know that. But I don't really know why.*

After Andre agrees to initiate this kind of conversation with his wife, the counselor provides encouragement to Andre for his willingness to take this step by highlighting his humbleness to admit to her, "I don't know why you're angry." The counselor acknowledges the courage it takes to ask the question and also prepares Andre to respond well to his wife's response, noting that approaching her in this way might feel unexpected to her because Andre has never pursued her in this way.

As a result of the counselor's encouragement to grow in understanding his wife's experience, Andre comes to know that his wife has reasons for her anger. After Andre has several conversations with his wife and then debriefs those conversations with his counselor, he is able to summarize the essence of his wife's concerns: "Our family life revolves around you and what you think and want. You rarely invite my voice into decision-making. I don't believe you even care about what I think."

Remember that the counselor doesn't have direct access to Andre's wife. And just as it would be a mistake to accept Andre's interpretation without testing the truth of it, the counselor should also not presume the wife sees or perceives everything accurately. We won't just blindly accept that her feedback about Andre is true. But this summary of her concerns does give Andre and his counselor a lot to explore, and Andre's heart and motivations for his marriage will be revealed in this process of exploration. Is he really willing to consider his wife's perspective? Is he willing to prayerfully consider whether there is truth to her words about him? Is he willing to repent and make changes if the Spirit convicts him of sin?

Andre is willing to consider her feedback so he and the counselor begin to wrestle through what Andre's wife has said. Here are some of the questions the counselor might use to explore this subject more deeply with Andre:

- Does anything resonate with you in her depictions of you?
- Let's consider a recent example to see if we can understand why she'd make a comment like: "You don't invite my voice into decision-making." Think of the last big decision you two made as a couple. How did that play out? Are there places you can see now that you could have been more collaborative with your wife?
- Do you value your wife's opinions? How do you show her that?
- How do you think you would feel toward someone if you believed they didn't care much about what you think?
- What is your understanding of the Bible's teaching on marriage—the goals, the purposes, the way it should be lived out—and how might that impact how you weigh your wife's feedback?

It is plain to see how the counseling might develop differently if they journey in this direction versus if the counselor had simply agreed with Andre's original interpretation.

At the risk of sounding redundant, I will say this again because it is so important: We will not interpret what the real needs are if we don't know the person. And we will not be able to journey toward a biblical interpretation together with the person if the person doesn't trust us. However, if we do know the person and their circumstances, and we have the person's trust, then we can together discern and interpret what is going on.

In Andre's case, let's say he came to a point where he felt compelled to take responsibility for ways he had unwittingly been self-centered in his marriage. His was not high-handed sin. He lacked insight into himself. He lacked insight into how his wife experienced him. He hadn't been intentionally cutting his wife from decision-making. However, if Andre is truly in counseling to explore how God might want him to grow, if he desires a marriage that is God-honoring, and if he desires to be a husband who shows interest in his wife's perspectives, then sound biblical counseling will help him grow.

Now let's consider how the counselor's process with Andre has been biblical so far. First, the counselor has been slow to arrive at conclusions. It would have been easy to agree with Andre's interpretation and forego the harder work of uncovering some of Andre's weaknesses and failures. But going slow is wise because the human heart—Andre's heart—is deep waters, and it takes time to draw it out (Proverbs 20:5). Going slow is wise because God calls us to sober judgment and a humble mind (Romans 12:3; 1 Peter 3:8). We are sobered when we remember that we as biblical counselors work in the name of the Lord— and we don't want to lead our brothers or sisters to stumble! Hasty conclusions put our counselees in danger of succumbing to a false interpretation. We are humble when we remember that we are not God and we can't see or fully know as God sees and knows (Proverbs 15:3)—and we want to walk with people in a way that reflects our limited ability to see and know.

Andre's counselor has been biblical by asking him questions that explore God's priorities for his people to walk in the Spirit (see Galatians 5:16–25). The bulleted list of questions given earlier in the chapter help Andre to wrestle with the following matters: Am I really seeking unity, and not division, with my wife? Am I committed to not being conceited and admitting my flaws and failures? Do I desire to walk with the Spirit more than I desire to be right or be perceived as the better spouse?

By leading Andre to consider such biblical priorities, the counselor is representing and joining the One who searches our hearts, who asks us all, at all times and in all the situations we are in, "Who do you love?" (Luke 10:27). He asks, "Are you a true worshiper of me or something else?" (Luke 4:8; John 4:23–24). He asks, "Will you submit to my authority?" (James 4:7).[3] By going slow and asking searching questions, the counselor shows an understanding of the human heart—of our temptations to stray, self-deceive, self-justify, defend ourselves, play it safe, and seek our own comfort rather than serve others in sacrificial love. And when our counselees are willing to be searched out in this way, then good things can happen.

So after many conversations with his wife and counselor, through the process of growing in self-understanding, through the Word's piercing of his thoughts and intentions (Hebrews 4:12), this is the interpretation that Andre came to: *I have sought to be a faithful, loving husband. But I have often failed to seek to understand my wife and have overlooked her thoughts and desires in ways that have been hurtful to her. I am called to grow in how I love my wife.*

With this interpretation, let me highlight that our interpretations must comport and agree with biblical priorities and

3. For an extensive list of questions that capture ways to explore who or what we are truly serving and worshiping, see David Powlison, "X-Ray Questions: Drawing out the Whys and Wherefores of Human Behavior," *Journal of Biblical Counseling* 18, no. 1 (Fall 1999): 2–8.

realities. Remember St. Augustine and Proverbs 14:12? We won't interpret rightly on our own. Our way may seem right, but we often don't get it right. We need an objective standard that comes from outside of ourselves. We need God to tell us what reality is. He calls us to conform to his ways, which requires us to know his ways and how he views reality. Only then can we be a faithful guide to our counselees. Many times, arriving at an accurate interpretation can involve using Scripture creatively in counseling conversations. I'll offer examples of how you can do so in chapters 9 and 10.

The ability to capture the interpretation in biblical categories gives us confidence that we are headed in a direction that honors the Lord and is therefore helpful for Andre (and his wife!). Might more be going on in his marriage than what Andre's interpretation captures? Most likely. What about how his wife is handling her anger? The way Andre describes her makes it sound like she is sinning. That may well be. But we have to work with what we know and work on what we can. Counseling doesn't usually address people's lives in a comprehensive way. We are limited by many factors. In this case, the counselor can't work with his wife because she hasn't come to counseling. We have to work with what God has allowed to emerge now. If God has led Andre to see ways he has been, and can be, self-centered, especially when it comes to decision-making, then we have a counseling agenda for now. Even as we realize that there are likely other, related concerns, this agenda is a worthwhile one because Andre is compelled and motivated by it and because we can both link it directly to biblical categories.

What biblical categories does Andre's interpretation represent? Here is the interpretation again: *I have sought to be a faithful, loving husband. But I have often failed to seek to understand my wife and have overlooked her thoughts and desires in ways that have been hurtful to her. I am called to grow in how I love my wife.*

These are some biblical categories that undergird this interpretation:

- We are all a mixed bag—made in God's image yet sinful and suffering. We are complex people. Andre cares about his marriage and has put forth effort. We can't paint him with one broad stroke. But there are ways, too, he has been blind to his treatment of his wife.
- *I am called to grow* is a biblical category. We are not perfect yet. God has begun the good work, but it isn't yet complete (Philippians 1:6). We are running our race, and we must keep running. Identifying areas of growth is an ongoing task of the Christian.
- God calls us to humbly consider one another (Philippians 2:3). Andre doesn't have the liberty to ignore his wife's concerns and experiences of him. His interpretation reflects his convictions that he has heard his wife and has prayerfully considered the possibility that she has perceived something true of him.
- God calls his people to repentance (1 John 1:9). Andre must confess his sin to God and to his wife and commit to a new way forward.

A new way forward. This brings us to the second major task of the middle of the counseling process: we imagine with people a new, biblically faithful way forward. We will turn there next.

Chapter 8

IMAGINING THE FAITHFUL WAY FORWARD

This is perhaps the most exciting and inspired part of the counseling process! It is God's mercy and grace to us that we can pursue a new way forward. Because God has made us alive in Christ through the forgiveness of sins (Colossians 2:13), we are a heaven-bound people, persevering to fully attain our prize, who is Christ (Philippians 3:14). What is ahead is better than what is behind, and so we press forward. With the Spirit's help, we seek to do the Father's will now on earth, even as it is now being done in heaven. These spiritual truths and realities all undergird the task of imagining the faithful way forward with our counselees.

Before we dive into the details of this part of the process, let me note that what I am referring to as the "imagined way forward" could also be called the "counseling plan." I am using "imagine" language instead because I find it more inspiring! How so? Because God endowed us with this powerful capability to imagine, to "look" beyond what is currently in our experiences and envision something more, something greater, and even glorious.

For the Christian, we must use our imaginations to envision our lives changing, developing, and maturing more and more into the likeness of Jesus. God stirs up our hearts with that which stirs up his heart—to bring beauty from our ashes, to replace oldness with newness—and that gives us vision, direction, and purpose in our lives. And because he has given us the Spirit, we can act on these imaginations and can work toward bringing them into our lived experience. So in counseling you consider together how your counselee can be stirred up to love and good works in the area that needs help (Hebrews 10:24). To be stirred up in this way, you will have to use your imaginations because counselees are in need of something new happening. With God's help, with the Spirit's power, redemptive imagining can get them there.

IMAGINE

Once you and the counselee have identified a biblical interpretation of the problem or issue, that interpretation sets the stage for them to imagine changes and begin acting on changes. This might be the longest point of the process, depending on the counselee's ease with making meaningful changes. Sometimes it will take people several weeks to demonstrate this, and sometimes it can take several years. Most people will fall somewhere in between, but this depends on many factors, such as the nature of the problem, the depth and complexity of the imagined way forward, the person's level of ability and spiritual maturity, and the resources present in the person's life.[1]

---

1. The American Counseling Association (ACA) code of ethics captures this same idea nicely with slightly different terms. It reads, "Counselors and their clients work jointly in devising counseling plans that offer reasonable promise of success and are consistent with the abilities, temperament, developmental level, and circumstances of clients." https://www.counseling.org/resources/aca-code-of-ethics.pdf, p. 4.

As we think about the process of conversing with our counselees and stirring up their imaginations, what guides our imagination? We start with Christ. How do his life, death, and resurrection shape our grasp of what God calls his people to? What does the Spirit—our Helper—help us to do? The interpretation has led us to confidence about how the Word speaks about the kinds of matters that are relevant to the person's situation, and now we are applying biblical wisdom to discern where to go from here.

Perhaps one of the most effective ways to imagine is to spend time with counselees reflecting together on who Jesus is. How he lived. How he served. How he laid down his life. How he took it back up again. How he serves us today. The life of our Lord, the ways of our Lord—this is where we find motivation. This is how we draw from the past—Christ's past—to help us track our new way forward. *Be thou my vision.* We desire Jesus to be our vision for our futures. *Thou my best thought.* Jesus is our best thought for our futures. The task of imagining includes carrying Jesus, our best thought, into a vision of the future that has been shaped by his life and love.

To think concretely about the task of imagining, let's return to our counseling example from the previous chapter and pretend again that the counselor and Andre had come to a *wrong* interpretation of his marriage. They both are in agreement that living with an angry wife is a burden, and this now leads to a wrong imagination. Misstep leads to misstep: the counselor helps Andre find solace in Proverbs 21:19—"better to live in a wilderness than with an angry wife." The counselor extends the verse as a way to start to imagine a flawed way forward based on their incorrect interpretation. Because of his Christian faith, Andre can't and won't leave his wife, but how can he find "better" ways to live since he has to live with a hot-tempered wife?

They start to imagine together what this could look like. The counselor recommends Andre find sources of fulfillment and joy outside of his marriage. This will help Andre persevere in staying in the marriage, which is one of his goals. Andre loves tennis, but he hasn't invested in this activity in many years, and so they imagine what steps he could take now to enjoy this hobby again. They imagine the difference it would make to Andre's experience if he were to pursue tennis. Andre feels cared for, known, and motivated to engage in this new way forward. He begins to feel justified in having his focus outside of the home to help ameliorate the suffering in his marriage. He is thinking about his marriage less and thinking about tennis more. This feels like a relief to him. After all, living with an angry wife is a form of suffering.

Andre is feeling more positive about his life, but has he really grown as a husband? Is his marriage any better now than it had been? The answer to both questions is no. We should want more for Andre. Tennis is a pittance compared to the changes God can do in him and in his marriage.

Now let's flip it again and play out what could happen if the counselor and Andre imagine a way forward based on an accurate interpretation of what is happening in his marriage. Andre's new interpretation helps him see that God's call on his life right now is to grow in calling forth his wife's viewpoints. How could this happen? Here is a summary of their conversations and the insights that helped Andre imagine the way forward.

Andre began to notice the differences between his and his wife's personalities and how he did seem to take up much more metaphorical "room" than she did. He came to understand himself more. He was an outgoing man, sharp and witty. He was quick to speak, quick to laugh, quick to joke, quick to draw conclusions, quick to make decisions. He started to perceive how his attributes could feel overwhelming for his wife and even lead him to unintentionally steamroll over her in their conversations. This made him realize he had been missing out on knowing his wife more fully. He imagined slowing himself down. He imagined asking for her thoughts on matters big and small—and he started to feel excited to see what he might discover!

Based on insights that Andre gained in counseling, here is a summary of his imagined way forward, put in his words: *I repent of overlooking my wife. I want to grow in making more space for her thoughts, feelings, and opinions to come out. To do this, I remember first how Christ has not overlooked me and how he makes space for me to share myself with him. I will pattern myself after Christ's love and, with God's help, work on asking my wife questions to draw her out, biting my own tongue, even tempering my personality for her sake. I will affirm with my words and by my actions that I want to know and understand her more.*

Indeed, this is a worthwhile way forward. Andre's imaginations here intertwine Christ's love with God's call for him to love. His imaginations are beginning to think practically and concretely about how to demonstrate that love and live it out.

As we did with the interpretive task, we want to be sure we can capture the imagined way forward with biblical categories. This gives us confidence in the way forward. These are the biblical categories that undergird Andre's way forward:

- We are made in God's image, and we each have unique creational abilities and gifts (Genesis 1:27; Psalm 139:14). Christians have spiritual gifts as well (1 Corinthians 12:4–8). This gives Andre good reason to pursue his wife's viewpoints. She has something to offer him.
- Even nonmoral attributes, like personality traits, must be submitted to the law of love. Love will at times require us

to reign in our natural ways of relating to others. This is why growing in self-understanding is so important for Christians: as we know ourselves more, we are better poised to *love others* (1 Corinthians 8:13; 10:23). We leverage our strengths for the benefit of others. Aware of our weaknesses, we are proactive to shield others from bearing the burden of them.

- God calls his people to repentance. Andre had been unknowingly sinning against his wife. He had committed sins of omission—failures to include, elicit, and pursue his wife to create a more collaborative partnership between them. He had failed to put himself in his wife's shoes and imagine how it might feel for her to relate and respond to someone with his type of personality.

- God desires Christian marriages to be unified (Matthew 19:6; Colossians 3:14). Unity is one fruit of Andre taking his wife's concerns and experiences to heart and proving by his actions that he hears her and wants to hear her.

Having imagined this way forward, Andre is ready to start making changes in his relationship with his wife. As I mentioned earlier in the chapter, this is where you go once the counselee has imagined that direction for the faithful way forward. You help counselees identify small, feasible steps that will enact the changes of the imagined way forward. Between sessions, they can work on and practice living out the first step. When they come to the next session, you follow up, asking, "How did it go? What went well? What was hard?"

Based on feedback, you and the counselee weigh whether the small step had been a reasonable one after it has been tested in real life. If it was challenging and not mastered, then you can try it again, perhaps with a tweak or adjustment to it. If it was mastered, then you work to identify the next step. The counselee is iterating and building on changes, then iterating again and building further. In counseling, you press the conversation forward: What can the counselee work on between now and the next session?

Identifying steps is a collaborative activity. By this point you know the person well, and you use that knowledge to agree on steps that are feasible and practical for the counselee to carry out. These steps are concrete and realistic in light of the person's struggle, context, and goals. They are personal steps in that sense. This is a personal, adaptable process, so the imagined way forward and what steps should be taken to act on that are going to look different for everyone, even if their issues are similar.[2]

In Andre's example, one aspect of his imagined way forward will be interacting with his wife about the steps he is taking. What does she think? To operate as a united couple, they must begin collaborating on what decision-making will look like between them. This is one way for Andre to demonstrate repentance, a way for him to truly pursue oneness in his relationship with his wife. This has been his wife's desire and has become his as well.

It would not be helpful to Andre's goals for the counselor to prescribe the way forward or for Andre to decide on all of the changes he wants to make on his own, even if that way forward or those changes seem good and right. The way forward must be personal and adapted to the people involved. One aspect of the counselor's job at this point in the process with Andre is to encourage him to pursue open, honest discussions with his wife.

---

2. Here is how the ACA code of ethics captures these ideas: "Counselors and clients regularly revise counseling plans to assess their continued viability and effectiveness, respecting clients' freedom of choice." https://www.counseling.org/resources/aca-code-of-ethics.pdf, p. 4.

The counselor can suggest that Andre initiate this collaborative process with his wife. We want to see Andre brainstorming with her, identifying together their values and the priorities that can help guide them in shared decision-making. We want to see them name changes together, changes that both honor the Lord and honor one another by enacting personalized love that is based on their newly informed understanding of each other.

As this is occurring between Andre and his wife at home, the counselor continues in session to provide a place for Andre to process how it is going. The counselor provides encouragement and continues to brainstorm with Andre about how to further build and improve upon what he, and now also his wife, imagine for how their particular marriage—with its particular set of gifts, strengths, and weaknesses—can reflect the unity that the Lord calls them to.

CONCLUSION

The middle of the counseling process is heading toward its close when the counselee has demonstrated the motivation and ability to consistently walk on the imagined way forward. Leading up to and as this is happening, your role is to provide follow-up, support, and accountability. You troubleshoot when bumps, twists, and turns arise along the new way. You pray together for God's strength and help—in the specific ways that the counselee needs it. Change isn't easy, and you normalize that if this is your counselee's experience. You encourage dependence on the Spirit. You point out evidence of the Spirit's work that you see. You collaborate together to identify what is next on this way forward.

Finally, note that the tasks of interpretation and imagination are needed for all the areas that the person wants to address in counseling. And the goals of counseling will have now been captured and expressed in the imagined way(s) forward. Andre had come in with vague counseling goals. His marriage was suffering, and he was hurting. His understanding of himself and his wife was so limited at that point that he could only express a goal of a "better marriage." As he and the counselor came to a greater understanding of him and his marriage, the goals were captured in the imagined way forward. Counseling goals grow and change according to the biblical interpretation of the problem and how that sets the agenda for the faithful imagined way forward.

Chapter 9

AN EXAMPLE OF USING SCRIPTURE IN COUNSELING

Connecting Jesus to the people we counsel is a regular joy in our biblical counseling practice! Scripture is alive because Jesus, the Word made flesh, is alive. And he is active in our lives in large and small matters. He speaks, encourages, admonishes, disciples, disciplines, and heartens us through his Word.

I often turn to the gospels when I counsel because our faith centers on Jesus—who he is, what he has done, what he will do. I do this because the gospels show Jesus's interactions with people. It is fascinating to watch God-in-the-flesh up close. It is vital for all of us to encounter Jesus again and again, so we are reminded what he is really like. We need to watch how he talks to people. Overhear what he says. See how he approaches people in their brokenness, confusion, sinfulness, and faith.

In this chapter, I will provide one example of a creative way you can use Scripture to lead people to an encounter with the living Jesus. As just one example, think of this chapter as priming the pump for you to consider how you use Scripture in counseling. Do you tend toward certain passages? What passages have proven especially helpful for particular problems? The resources page also points you to places that will expand your skill in applying Scripture in counseling.

AN ENCOUNTER WITH JESUS

I find counselees are often surprised by what they see in the gospel accounts. Why? We all have misconceptions about God and misinterpretations about God. We tend to assume how Jesus will respond in a situation. We think we know how he will treat broken, sinful people. We assume we know how he will deal with us. Our perceptions color what we believe about how he will deal with me and how he will deal with you. The stories correct these misconceptions.

When I turn to the gospels to get a glimpse of Jesus up close, I often frame a passage with the question, "What does this interaction show us about what Jesus is *really* like?" One woman I met with tended to fall into the trap of thinking that Jesus was disgusted with her because of her past sins. She needed a fresh encounter with Jesus. She needed a reminder of what he is really like. We read Luke 5:27–28 together: "After this he went out and saw a tax collector named Levi, sitting at the tax booth. And he said to him, 'Follow me.' And leaving everything, he rose and followed him."

Before we talked about the passage, I shared with her how tax collectors in Israel were hated. To fully appreciate Jesus's invitation, it's important to understand how utterly undesirable Levi was as a person. Tax collectors were known as crooks that conspired with the despised Roman officials. Their thievery actually made them ineligible to participate in Jewish religious life. All this makes Jesus's invitation astonishing.

With this background information in mind, we can help someone think through Jesus's encounter with Levi using the following questions:

- What do you think Levi was doing, thinking, and feeling as he sat in his tax booth?
- Why do you think Jesus wants a tax collector to be his disciple?
- What must it have been like for Levi to receive this invitation from Jesus?
- How does it strike you that Jesus gives this invitation to a tax collector?
- What do you make of Levi's response?

It can be fruitful to discuss this last question. Levi—better known as Matthew, the author of the gospel bearing his name—responded in a remarkable way. It seems he didn't hesitate for a moment. It appears he abandoned his sordid career without a second thought. And after immediately following Jesus out of his booth, the next sentence tells us that he had a great feast in his house with Jesus as the guest of honor. Levi was celebratory. He fully allowed himself to revel in Jesus's company. There is no sense that Levi's shameful past followed him when he decided to follow Jesus.

Though Levi's response to Jesus was decisive, your counselee's response will likely be different. Luke 5:27–28 is a conversion story and, in Levi's case, a direct call to ministry. If the person you are meeting with has not yet professed faith in Christ, you certainly could use this verse to explore the person's reaction to Christ's gracious call to repent. But I mostly use it with believers because we all struggle to follow Jesus in certain ways. The struggle could be due to sin. Or it can be due to brokenness.

For the woman I was meeting with, it was the latter. She had repented of a sinful past many years ago, but she still lived with a heavy burden of shame. And because she identified herself by her past, she thought Jesus identified her that way too. Seeing Jesus call a tax collector to be his disciple caused her to rethink what he might say about her sinful past and her present identity.

So rather than making Levi a model to follow, focus instead on Jesus's invitation—which comes to us all in a personally relevant way. Describe a Levi-like scene, personalized with details to fit the individual's version of a "tax booth." Name the area of sin, suffering, or brokenness that the person is struggling with.

> **Counselor:** There you are. Sitting out in the open, just as Levi was. The thing you most don't want people to know about you [speak here about the person's particular struggle or sin] is out there for the world to see. You feel ugly because of it, completely disgraced. Yet Jesus is approaching you. He comes up to you. He is not repulsed by you, even though he sees you as you really are. He knows how you have sinned. He understands the ways you have been battered by the brokenness of this world. He talks to you. He says, "Follow me and be my disciple." What is that like for you? With where you are today in this struggle, how are you going to respond? What are you going to say? What are you going to do?

The responses to Jesus's invitation could be endless. Here are some you might hear:

- "I want to run away when I see Jesus coming toward me because I'm afraid of what he is going to say."
- "I want to ask Jesus why he wants me to follow him."

- "How can I be a disciple when my life is such a mess?"
- "I want to follow him! But I don't think I can really leave my past behind me like Levi did. It will always haunt me."
- "I don't think this invitation can be for me. I don't believe Jesus really wants me to follow him."

Let people talk it out. Make it safe for people to reflect honestly about their gut reactions to receiving a personal invitation from Jesus Christ.

People's reactions will differ. The woman I was counseling felt she had to clean up her "tax booth" before Jesus reached her. She wanted to make sure her tax booth looked a certain way so that Jesus would want to invite her to go with him. Though people's responses will vary to this invitation, Jesus is the same yesterday, today and tomorrow. After you have spent time exploring and processing your counselee's reactions, you will also have an opportunity to share what Jesus is really like. This is always good news. For my counselee, the good news was that Jesus sees her mess and he calls her to himself anyway. She doesn't have to carry the burden of cleaning herself up; in fact, she can't do that. Jesus is the one who washes away her sinfulness. And because he does, she can rest in his finished work. She is now who *he* says she is—a beloved, spotless daughter. This passage paved the way for her to rightly interpret how God sees her. And repentant faith is for her to now trust that Jesus's view of her is the one he wants her to adopt about herself. Her way forward was to honor Christ by following *his* lead in what he says is true about her. Her way forward was to trust and believe that he is the one who gets it right about who she really is.

With this new, biblical interpretation about how Christ responds to sinful people, we started to imagine what life for her would be like if shame did not have the last word. We started to imagine what it would feel like if Jesus gets the last word about her past and who she is today. How would Jesus's interpretation make a difference in how she relates to God? What about how she relates to others? How would her marriage and the way she relates to her husband be impacted by Jesus's covering of her shame? We explored questions like these, catching a vision for the changes God could bring about and the ways she could act on those changes.

Chapter 10

A CASE STUDY IN THE MIDDLE: NADIA

In this chapter, I will highlight how the major tasks of the middle of the counseling process unfolded in my work with Nadia, with a focus on how the use of two Scripture passages helped us to faithfully interpret and imagine.

INTERPRET

After several weeks of Nadia bringing in the most recent event at work that caused her to panic, a pattern emerged. Nadia was crippled under the weight of her own unrealistic expectations. The causes for Nadia's panic were truly small matters. They didn't feel that way to her, but as she shared them with me, I was able to offer her a more objective perspective. For example, she had one day recorded a detail of a patient's medical history incorrectly. I asked more questions until I understood the following: There was no harm done. She had realized her mistake that same day and had corrected it immediately. She hadn't gotten in trouble for this; no one had even realized it except her! Even if the error had gone uncorrected, no harm would have come to the patient. It was truly an inconsequential mistake, and would have been considered as such by Nadia's colleagues, given what she knew about the workplace.

Yet that is not how Nadia experienced it. She was panicked about it for several hours that day, and it had not been easy for her to shake that feeling. That was the pattern that emerged from her examples: objectively small issues garnered a big panic reaction from her. A summary of what emerged in our counseling was that *Nadia set impossibly high standards for herself*, and she had historically done very well at hitting high standards. She was brilliant, a natural student, and already regarded as a gifted doctor. Hard things came easily to her. But to her dismay, she wasn't perfect and was undone in times when she saw any sign of weakness.

As a way to help her process what she was doing, we did an exercise on the whiteboard. As I counsel, I keep an erasable whiteboard beside me. I often find it helpful to visually record aspects of our conversation. With Nadia, I wrote out a paraphrase of a portion of John 16:33: "In this world you will have trials and sorrows. . . ." I then asked her to fill in her usual response to hardship or seeing her weaknesses. She said that her inclination was to study longer, pursue more information, and push herself harder. She expected that she should find a way through any trial she faced. Other people might have difficulties, but if she was just savvy and quick thinking enough, she thought she could escape troubles. After all, troubles shouldn't exist if you are doing things right. I wrote her answers on the board as she talked.

Next, I read aloud how Jesus finished his thought. "But be of good cheer. I have overcome the world" (AMPC).

Jesus's words enabled me to graciously help her interpret what she was doing and then to deliver the good news of how God could help her escape her self-imposed standards. Her version of "good cheer" only came when *she* found her own way to overcome her hardship or strengthen her perceived weakness. But she realized that wasn't "good cheer" at all! God used this verse as one way to help her loosen the grip of her self-inflicted standards. She began to understand that even though she can't be perfect and coast through life without facing real limitations, she has a God who nonetheless gives her reasons to be glad. What are those reasons? Why can she be imperfect and still be okay? What does it look like to find peace in Jesus and to delight in his perfection instead of striving for her own? We explored questions like these together.

To build upon ways she was starting to see God, herself, and her panic differently, we discussed Psalm 103:13–14 in another session. I've found that this passage helps with those who lean toward legalism—Christians who gauge their relationship with God by their achievement, those who set impossibly high standards for themselves, as in Nadia's case, or those who struggle with perfectionism. These verses tell us, "As a father shows compassion to his children, so the LORD shows compassion to those who fear him. For he knows our frame; he remembers that we are dust" (Psalm 103:13–14).

I spoke about these words by starting with our "dustiness" in verse 14 and then moving backward into the Lord's compassion from verse 13. To provide you with some insight into our conversation, the next few paragraphs contain some of my talking points. Please keep in mind, however, that I did not give Nadia a monologue! These concepts were simply starting points for my conversation and interaction with her.

These verses give us an accurate view of ourselves. We are dust. Is dust strong? No. Can dust stand firm? No. Can dust fight well? No. All these things are true of you. And God knows it. God knows your frame. So when God sees that you are easily shaken, like dust, he has compassion on you. He doesn't set impossible expectations for you because how could dust live up to those expectations? It can't. We can't. Even without sin, we could never live up to the expectation of self-sufficiency because God made us to be dependent.

You don't need to endlessly berate yourself for being imperfect. Do you know why? Because Christ has lived up to the highest expectations for you. God knows your frame well. He knows that you would never be able to live as anything but powerless dust needing his animating strength. But he was also so utterly moved by your weak frame that he sent his Son to save you, and he sends his Spirit to sustain you.

Now you are in Christ. In Christ you have a secure standing before the Father that hasn't been earned by you. Christ earned it for you. You couldn't earn it, and you still can't earn it. That gives you permission to struggle. Permission to be weak. Permission to get it wrong and to still come back to him. Permission to be dust. And this struggling is actually a sign that dust might be coming to life because dust couldn't even struggle were it not for the Father's strong, intervening hand in its life. Dust would just be dust.

So when you fail, when you see your weaknesses, know that your Father does not define you as a failure. Instead, as you stumble and trip, he still looks on you with compassion. He picks you up, shakes the dust off of you, and puts you back on the path he is leading you along, a path that he is on with you. In fact, it's a path you wouldn't even be on were it not for him putting you on it. So be weak on this journey because your strong Father is with you and patient with you. Be humbled. You are dust. But your Father remembers that. And so can you.

These verses complemented our conversation about John 16:33. They worked together to make Jesus the strong hero. Nadia doesn't have to be the strong hero. She is a capable, gifted young woman. But she is a person. And her weaknesses create an opportunity for her to remember her need to run to her strong Savior.

As we think about how I used the psalm with Nadia, consider this statement from David Powlison: "The task in any ministry moment is to choose [and] emphasize . . . a truth for the sake of relevant application to particular persons and situations. You can't say everything all at once—and you shouldn't try. Say one relevant thing at a time."[1]

The truth I chose to emphasize for Nadia is that she is dust. Dust isn't the comprehensive way to understand the human condition—it's one way—but it was not yet a category Nadia had for herself. In light of her striving for perfection, it was relevant for her to hear that she is dust to help her calibrate the kinds of expectations she should have for herself. It was relevant for her to hear that she is dust to help her calibrate the kinds of expectations God has for her. Accepting she was dust brought her freedom. Learning to rest in God's strength instead of her own brought her peace.

Here is a combined summary on how she came to both interpret her panic and then imagine a faithful way forward: *God has gifted me in many ways, and when I encounter my limitations, it crushes me. I panic when I see that I am truly dust. But the*

---

1. David Powlison, "How Does Sanctification Work? (Part 1)," *Journal of Biblical Counseling* 27, no. 1 (2013): 54.

Lord is the only one who is truly strong and perfect, and I am learning contented dependence on him instead of depending on my own capabilities. When I see evidence that I am dust, I will remember God has compassion for me. Though I am tempted to feel disdain for myself in those moments, he does not disdain me. More than that, he has overcome the world for me so I will rest in his finished work instead of relying on myself to overcome the hard things I face.

Notice that there is repentance in her understanding. God's kindness—her seeing his great compassion for her in her weaknesses—led to her repentance (Romans 2:4). She was able to see that there was pride in her thinking that she could or should be perfect. Only God is perfect. Before, it would have been bad news to hear that she couldn't be perfect because that had been her version of her good cheer. However, we knew she was growing because it started to sound like good news. It became a relief. She can't be perfect. God's perfection became a balm to her panic. She had a new way to engage with her panic. God's perfection and his mercy toward her imperfection was a refuge she could run to when the panic started to rise.

We imagined together a quick prayer that she could pray at work whenever panic came: "God, you alone are perfect, and I rest in you. Help me to address this situation, accept my limitations, and be okay even if it doesn't turn out okay." Seeking God in those moments where she felt her vulnerability or encountered her weakness was an action step she began to take at work. It was a silent prayer, a quick way for her to reorient herself to her God and remember what is most important in those moments. This was the first step on the way forward that she practiced in real life.

It proved helpful. She remembered to pray, and her new categories for understanding herself and God helped her let it go when she made a mistake.

Since the prayer was helpful, we added a new step to build upon it. We imagined her writing down on a piece of paper a brief shorthand reminder of the interpretation: *You are dust, and God gets that.* Nadia would keep it in her pocket and look at it as needed. This, too, helped her. She discovered that reading the note at the beginning of her workday helped establish her mindset as she began her work.

After several sessions of her implementing the imagined way forward, she was experiencing less panic at work. When panic did come, she was able to move through it more quickly and get to a sense of resolve in her thoughts and emotions.

Chapter 11

CONSIDERATIONS IN THE MIDDLE

As in chapter 6, here is a list of questions to help you reflect when you are in the middle of the counseling process. These considerations might not work themselves out in actual conversations with the person, but they are intended to provide you with a chance to slow down and be thoughtful, self-reflective, and prayerful as you do the work in the middle. The questions are in no particular order.

1. *How are you experiencing this person now?* Do you look forward to your meetings with this person? Why or why not? For example, sometimes when I have dreaded meeting with someone, it was due to feeling overwhelmed with their situation; somehow it felt hopeless to me. This feeling is good to both acknowledege honestly and to talk over with a supervisor.

2. *As you have experienced this person during several weeks, do you notice that you are making any assumptions?* Have you made assumptions about them, about what you think is happening, about what you think is best for them? How

are you checking on those assumptions and keeping them in check?

3. *Have you brought your case to a consultation group or supervisor to gain others' insights for interpretation and which biblical truths apply?* You are considering what Scripture verses, passages, and narratives apply to your counselee's concerns and what ways you can creatively make connections. As you are working on the major task of interpretation, this is an important time to get input from others.

4. *How has counseling helped your counselee move toward their goals so far?* Initiate a conversation with your counselee about their goals. What has been helpful? Has anything been unhelpful? Talk about their sense of progress with the desired goals and outcomes for counseling. What is your sense of the progress your counselee has made? One way to consider this is to think about where you are in interpreting biblically the concerns you and the counselee are working on. Is it becoming clearer how the Bible and biblical wisdom makes sense of the concerns and how that paves the way to imagine the faithful way forward?

5. *Are there ways you can be creative in the counseling room?* Does any music, literature, or art connect to problems you and the counselee are discussing? Though counseling adults primarily entails conversations, there are times when mixing things up can help get a message across more effectively. In addition, there are types of people who are more aesthetically inclined and can consider ideas and concepts more readily through creative means. Feel free to think creatively with all the unique tools and means God has provided in his creation. Two examples from

my counseling come to mind. One was with a depressed counselee who struggled with reflecting on how she was doing week to week. Updating me on her week sent her into a discouraging spiral of overanalysis. For a time, we decided to forego conversations that relied on her processing her progress and use that time to listen to and discuss a hymn. I'd print out the lyrics ahead of time, and we'd listen and then reflect together on the lyrics. She appreciated the change of focus and the opportunity the hymns gave her to set her mind on things above (Colossians 3:1).

In another case, a counselee struggled mightily with shame, making it difficult for this individual to receive God's personal love. Because the message of God's forgiveness was hard to get through, I tried to think outside the box. One time I gave this counselee a children's story to ponder between sessions. The story told of a persistent mouse doggedly pursuing a bear for companionship, despite the bear's rebuffs. As a metaphor, we spoke of this counselee as the bear in the story and the Holy Spirit as the mouse. It was my hope and prayer that the message coming in a surprising, unexpected way would get through to my counselee better than talking alone.

6. *"How are we doing?"* This is a question I often pose in the middle of the counseling process. As we've discussed earlier, the relationship itself is influential, and if there is anything amiss relationally this kind of question can help bring it out so you can talk about it and work through it together. Have you checked in recently about how the relationship is developing between you and the counselee? Because your role as the counselor carries a level of authority, the counselee might not bring this up. Sometimes I'll offer a general comment to establish

and affirm that I view our counseling time as space to practice working through misunderstandings or differing viewpoints in a way that honors the Lord. Many, many people struggle with this in their personal lives, and the counseling room can be a safe space to practice having conversations that are interpersonally uncomfortable. You want to be that safe, mature person who models godliness, which means you are humble, willing to seek forgiveness, and quick to listen to your counselee's concerns.

7. *Do you follow up after any hard conversations?* It's wise to check in with people after a conversation or session when you gave hard-to-hear feedback. For example, "Last time we met, I shared an observation I know was not easy for you to hear. I want to check in and see how you and I are doing after having that hard conversation." If the session ended on an especially difficult note, you might want to follow up sooner than the next session. Pursuing your counselee in these ways is a way to take care of the counseling relationship.

8. *Is there continuity in your times together?* Is it clear from session to session what you're working on and that the counseling is building on itself? Purposefulness and intentionality are characteristic traits of formal counseling. If it doesn't feel that way, this is a good time to initiate a conversation with the individual about your impression and to work together to clarify how your sessions can be best utilized to help the counselee.

THE END OF THE MIDDLE

Presumably, the middle part of the counseling process will be the longest. Depending on the person and what this person is working on in counseling, there may be one major interpretation and imagined way forward—as in Nadia's case. Others might have unrelated issues they want to address, so you may work together to interpret and imagine for each of those issues. Remember that in all conversations, you as the biblical counselor must be counted on to always think, interpret, and imagine in ways that comport with biblical realities. Doing so is one of the distinctions of a biblical counselor's work.

To summarize, the major tasks of the middle of the counseling process are to interpret what is happening in the counselee's life according to biblical truths and to be able to connect the interpretation with biblical categories. We imagine together a way forward that has been shaped by the life and love of our Savior. This imagined way forward will also connect to biblical categories and biblical priorities.

To consider these two tasks together, we could say that the desired outcome of the middle of the counseling process is for the counselee to possess this kind of sentiment: *I have come to an understanding of both my situation and how God is calling me to move forward. I have caught a vision for how Jesus's life paves the way for me to live my life in this area that has been hard and troublesome.*

As the counselee has now begun to walk this way forward, and has begun to experience success, you are approaching the end of a counseling season. We will turn there next.

Part 3:
The End of the
Counseling Process

The primary focus for the end of the counseling process is to set the counselee up well to continue interpreting and imagining biblically. Thus, the two major tasks at the end of the counseling process are to:

1. Recognize together, with confidence, that the counselee has a clear grasp of the way forward and the momentum and motivation to keep going, and
2. Send the counselee off with realistic expectations for continued growth and a long-term vision for the future.

Chapter 12

BUILDING MOMENTUM AND PERSEVERANCE

*"I instruct you in the way of wisdom and lead you
along straight paths."—Proverbs 4:11, NIV*

The Lord is faithful. He faithfully instructs us. He faithfully
leads us along. His ways are wise. His paths are straight. As you
near the end of counseling, you and your counselee have interpreted where the straight path is for them. You have imagined
what life is like for them on the straight path. And your counselee has submitted to the Lord's lead and begun to walk along
that path. At the end of the counseling process, you are bearing
witness to this happening. The counselee is bearing witness to it
happening. The counselee's troublesome behaviors or responses
have been changing. Sinful patterns have lost their grip in the
person's life. The person runs quickly to the Lord for comfort in
the midst of ongoing suffering. Doubt and unbelief have given
way to trust and rest in God's faithfulness—despite the circumstances. When we are in that place of our counseling, then the
end of counseling is near. This chapter will give you ideas to

consider as you weigh with your counselee whether it is time for counseling to end.

MEET LESS OFTEN

One of our jobs as biblical counselors is to work ourselves out of a job. Our greatest thought for people is Jesus. It is dependence on Jesus. It is satisfaction and fulfillment in Jesus. By implication, we don't want to create dependence on counseling or the counseling relationship. Our role in formal counseling settings is to come alongside others for a season and to equip them for faithful living in areas where they sought help. When you and the counselee are gaining confidence that the person has been equipped and can persevere in the imagined way forward, then it is a good idea to consider decreasing the frequency of sessions. It will come when you sense that counseling feels less needed, and your counselee probably will sense this too.

I encourage you to raise this topic, starting with a conversation about the frequency of your meetings. For example, I could say, "You should be so encouraged by the work you are doing in counseling. As you have shared with me, and as I have seen, you are working hard to implement in your life the changes we have talked about. I am so thankful for your progress. You might have been wondering—and I am too—if we are nearing the end of our season of counseling. One thing I have done with others when we have been in a similar place is to start meeting less frequently. That helps us see how things go when a longer stretch of time passes without you receiving counseling help. How would you feel about trying that for our next couple of sessions—perhaps just meeting once a month instead of biweekly?"

If people have been growing in confidence in their ability to enact new ways of living, then you can expect to hear agreement to the idea of meeting with decreased frequency. If the person disagrees, talk through the reasons why. If you proceed with decreased frequency, the longer stretch of time between sessions will be telling. It will tell you both how much more counseling help, if any, is needed. If counseling is still needed, you continue to iterate and fine-tune the steps of growth to practice in real life, keep troubleshooting as needed, while you continue to provide care, encouragement, and reinforcement of the imagined way forward.

IMAGINE THE LONG-TERM WAY FORWARD

As you near the end of counseling, it's also the time to initiate conversations that will help form and shape a long-term understanding and vision of the struggle and faithfulness to God amid the struggle. The imagined way forward has proved itself valid and helpful already in the short-term of this person's life. Now as you both see this growth, you will want to equip your counselees to persevere over the long-term. Knowing the nature of your counselee's struggle, what's a realistic arc for that struggle over time? This is especially important for matters related to ongoing suffering, for the kinds of circumstances that might not change or "get better" in this life. Often we will counsel people who will not have much change in the area that is hard—maybe it's chronic pain. Counseling is ending, and the pain is still there. Or maybe it's a failed relationship. Counseling is ending, and the relationship has not been restored. But what has changed, matured, and grown by the end of counseling is people's view of God in the midst of it. Their understanding of what God calls them to is changed. Their sense of what to expect over the long haul has been refined. On the last point, we again can help prepare people for this by naming wise, realistic expectations.

We can cast a vision and even preemptively help people interpret an experience that might come in the future, given the nature of the struggle. For example, with a failed relationship, you can help your counselee prepare for the future by starting a conversation like this: "When we've endured a significant loss, as you have, over time the pain of it can ebb and flow. As our season of counseling will come to a close soon, I know you feel more at peace with what happened, and I am grateful for that. But there might come a time when the pain of the loss feels acute again. Sometimes it's a transition in life. Something important is happening to you, and it hurts when you remember that you don't have this person anymore. I want you to know that that would be a normal feeling to have and doesn't mean that the work you've done to heal is all for naught."

In that same vein, you can prepare people who have made strides in fighting a pattern of sin by brainstorming a plan for a potential, future time if they were to fall back into old habits. This must be discussed sensitively and with hope because falling back is not inevitable. Yet if there is a plan in place for responding if it does occur, it's more likely the person won't fall so hard.

You can initiate a conversation that sounds similar to this: "It has been a joy to see how you have depended on the Spirit's help to fight against sin. You have strategies in place now to help deter and distract you when temptations come. I am so hopeful for how God will continue to show his faithfulness in this area as you abide in him. As we look toward the end of counseling, one thing I like to do with people is put a plan in place in case there comes a time in the future where you may feel strongly tempted or maybe you have given into temptation. Of course, we hope and pray that won't happen, but if we have a plan for what you'll do next, that can help you get back on track more quickly." From there you collaborate and agree on a plan with the counselee.

BE ALERT TO INDICATORS OF SPIRITUAL HEALTH

What else should you and the counselee be alert to as indications that counseling is nearing its end? In his article, "When Should Counseling End?" Alasdair Groves identifies four spiritual elements that you will want to know are active and vibrant in the counselee's life:

1. The presence of consistent spiritual disciplines
2. The involvement of at least one other person who is lovingly engaged
3. The ability to ask for specific prayer
4. Committed involvement in a church community[1]

In addition to the person having shown momentum and perseverance to traverse the faithful way forward, the presence of these four elements gives you and the counselee further reason to believe and hope that they will continue on the "straight path" after you step out of the counselee's life. This means you will assess and inquire about each of these four elements. I don't mean that you should do so all at once, as a sort of checklist to cover. Rather, over time as you are walking with the counselee, be alert to these matters because they point to spiritual health and spiritual depth. This also means you will work together to create or strengthen any areas that are lacking or weak. Nadia's case study will provide an example of this later.

CONCLUSION

Accurate knowledge of the matters we've discussed in this chapter will culminate in both you and the counselee feeling confident that the decision to end counseling is the right one. You

1. J. Alasdair Groves, "When Should Counseling End?" *The Journal of Biblical Counseling* 27, no. 3 (2013): 72–73.

will have identified and discussed concrete reasons for you and the counselee to trust that it is the right decision. The counselee feels equipped. The way forward has been clear for some time now, and your counselee has internal momentum and motivation to persevere.

When you and the counselee are at this point, then you are ready to say goodbye. The next chapter walks through an example of how to structure a last session that will send people off in ways that will bless them.

Chapter 13

THE LAST SESSION

When you and the counselee have your last session, here are some ideas to move through it in ways that honor the Lord and the individual. You can check in at the beginning of the session to see what is on the counselee's heart, and pursue a conversation about whatever that is. Then you should be prepared to reflect personally, celebrate the Lord's work, and close in prayer in this last meeting.

REFLECT PERSONALLY

As you head into a last session, prepare beforehand to offer some personal reflections. Prayerfully consider questions like these: What did you learn from your counselee? What fresh insights about God brought you delight through conversations with your counselee? What did you see in your counselee that you admire? How did the counselee encourage you, your faith, and your walk with the Lord?

For example, maybe there was a trait about the Lord that you had not considered in such an in-depth way but one that emerged as central to the person's interpretation and imagined way forward. Now is the time to share how you were blessed by reflecting on that trait together with the person. We know that God also does his loving, sanctifying work in us as counselors—albeit in a different way—but nonetheless we learn, we grow, we change. Where have you seen this? It will bless and encourage your counselee to hear it from you. This is a way to be personal.

CELEBRATE THE LORD'S WORK IN YOUR COUNSELEE'S LIFE

You have been pointing out the Spirit's activity in previous sessions, especially as the person has been making attempts and growing in strides on the imagined way forward. A last session is a time for you to now summarize what you have seen God do in and for your counselee. The sound, biblical interpretations and the faithful ways forward are a language you and the counselee speak fluently now. For the last time, you will summarize these for your counselee.

In your summary, speak to your counselee of the specific ways you saw the Holy Spirit at work and active. Calling forth such spiritual realities is a way to stir up faith in the Lord, who has been present throughout the counseling process. Continuing to build your counselee's faith in the Lord is important for their future endurance because he stays after we have said goodbye.

A last session is a time to speak freely about how you are thankful to God for the specific ways he's shown himself committed to your counselee's flourishing. It's a time for you to honor your counselee for whatever noble, praiseworthy thing you saw in them over the course of your time together—their hard work, commitment to God, courage, discipline, humbleness, curiosity. Whatever it was, be personal and build your counselee up (1 Thessalonians 5:11). It's a time to honor the Lord by speaking the ways he has proven himself faithful to your counselee throughout the counseling process.

Reaching out for help is a sign of health and strength, not weakness or failure. Your counselee did this in pursuing counseling, and framing it this way one last time is also a way to reinforce what would be a good response in the future if they should need help again. God made us dependent creatures, and he does not revile our need. That means there is nothing shameful about needing help. What matters is what we do next. These are ways you have helped your counselee think biblically about the nature of struggle, sin, and suffering, and you can preemptively cover shame by giving a last encouragement like this.

CLOSE IN PRAYER

You can close your session with a personal prayer. I like to thank God for the ways he guided the process, helping us grasp the interpretation and imagined way forward. I thank him for the ways he helped the person walk on the way forward and for his faithfulness and commitment to the person. Then I commit the person to the Lord. I gravitate toward the Numbers 6 blessing, and so I often pray that blessing for the counselee. I also entrust people into the Lord's care, which reflects that they are going from my life but that the Lord will remain with them.

Though you can and should pray in whatever way feels natural for you, I do think it is lovely to think of the goodbye and the closing prayer as an opportunity for you to *bless* your counselees as they go. To be prayed for is a blessing. To hear again in prayer how God has been faithful is a blessing. To hear reminders of God's faithfulness is a blessing. To receive an actual blessing from you is a gift.

As counseling has now ended for your counselee, our intention is that he or she is leaving your care with this kind of sentiment: *God has used counseling to grow me in the areas of concern. I have a nuanced, biblical understanding now of myself, the Lord, and the problem, and I feel equipped to walk in new ways over the long haul.*

AFTER THE LAST SESSION

Now is the time to care for your counselee through good administration. Finish up notes. Write a case summary. If the person ever seeks help again at the place where you counsel, a completed file could potentially help a new counselor benefit from the previous work you did with the person.

At the end of counseling, counselors at CCEF also write a "closure letter" that goes to the counselee and into their file. This closure letter serves practical purposes such as informing counselees that they can reach out for counseling help again if needed, and that they can also reach out if they are in need of a referral for help from another source.

I also use this letter as one last opportunity to be personal with my counselees. Because people can keep this letter if they so choose, I write a brief recap of the matters I summarized and celebrated in the last session. In the next chapter, I will show you my letter to Nadia.

CONCLUSION

The last session can raise many different emotions for either you, the counselee, or both! It is by and large a joyful time because of how the counselee has grown, and you take the time to speak together of how God has done this. It can also be sad because you are saying goodbye, and that is bittersweet. In formal counseling, it is often not known when or if you will see this person again. In these times, I take great comfort in our status as family members, family members with the same Father—a Father who has promised he will one day gather all of his children together. We will see one another again.

Chapter 14

A CASE STUDY AT THE END: NADIA

Nadia and I knew we were close to ending counseling as her panic experiences were decreasing both in frequency and in intensity. The tools we identified were providing help when she became anxious, and she was able to move through her anxieties more quickly and effectively when she grew concerned about something. Because she did not have other matters to address in counseling, we did not have much left to work on as we saw that she was having the kind of success she was hoping to have at work.

As Nadia made progress in her goal of reducing panic at work, I asked her to start to imagine how she could find support from others after counseling ended. Nadia identified two action steps. One, she would share with her small group about the struggle we had been addressing in counseling. She sees her small group regularly, so they would be able to pray with her. She could invite them to check in with her on how things had been going for her at work, and, even more importantly, they could ask her how she was doing in not erecting impossible standards for herself. Two, though she knew I had been willing to speak to her pastor, she was willing to do it herself. We agreed that it would be better for her relationship with her pastor if she were the one who shared her struggle and the specific ways she was now clinging to the Lord for help.

With these spiritual supports in place, and with Nadia doing well with fighting her panic with her new tools, it was easy to make the final decision to draw our counseling relationship to a close.

THE LAST SESSION WITH NADIA

REFLECT PERSONALLY

As I thought about how I had been blessed by my meetings with Nadia, I reflected on my admiration for Nadia's work in such a high-pressure, intense environment. I have never had to perform in that kind of environment, and I could only imagine how stressful it could become to have the health and well-being of people's lives in my hands. This helped me appreciate even more that, in the midst of her panic, she sought to find refuge in the shelter of her God. She could have run to thousands of places for relief and comfort, but she ran to her God. This was noble and praiseworthy, and so I shared this with her.

CELEBRATE THE LORD'S WORK

Nadia and I had a good laugh in our last session as we recalled her journey from setting impossibly standards to seeing herself as dust. There's a wide gap between the two, but the Lord brought her through it! So we laughed for how right it felt for the Lord to humble her, for her to be able to come to terms with her dependence on her God. It's a delight when we can let God have his rightful place and accept our place. We enjoyed together that this had happened in Nadia's heart.

CLOSING COMMENTS ABOUT NADIA'S CASE

To wrap up my counseling process with Nadia, let me make some final observations and tie up some loose ends.

NADIA'S PROCESS WAS STRAIGHTFORWARD

She did not come to counseling with far-reaching concerns in multiple areas of her life. I chose her case for this book because it had a clear beginning, middle, and end and, therefore, lent itself well as a teaching example. We only met about eight times, and that was enough to accomplish her goal for counseling. Not all cases are as clear-cut; in fact, most are not! However, for most cases the major tasks for each of the stages I have presented will be relevant and can be pursued.

NADIA SEVERAL TIMES HELPED ME UNDERSTAND HER RACIAL AND CULTURAL PERSPECTIVE

Because of our differences, Nadia did several times give me a cultural understanding of her experiences that helped give me context for what she was sharing. For example, there was one instance when Nadia wanted to speak about the racial differences with certain colleagues at work, and we talked through how this was affecting her.

And do you remember how Nadia shared her family's immigration story with me? Though it did not factor into our counseling in a significant way, I am thankful Nadia shared it with me because it did help me have a fuller picture of her, her past, her parents' influence, and her hopes for herself. It was a good use of our time because it helped me know her in a deeper way. It was a chance for her, too, to experience me taking an interest in her story and being curious about her culture, which was good for our relationship.

MY ASSUMPTIONS COULD HAVE HINDERED THE
COUNSELING PROCESS IF I HAD NOT HELD THEM IN CHECK

Upon self-reflection early in the counseling process, I became aware of an assumption that I had to keep in check throughout our counseling. My assumption was that Nadia's parents' desire for her to become a doctor connected to the high standards she had for herself. As I put myself in her shoes, I could see the possibility of pushing myself hard in order to please my parents. But that was *not* Nadia's experience, and I had to be careful not to assume my belief was true! In session, we explored the origins of Nadia's high standards, and I asked a couple of questions to see if there was a connection with her parents. Nadia did not make that connection. She described her parents as gracious, loving, and supportive, and she spoke of herself as the one who had devised impossibly high standards.

Why do I mention this? It is natural for us as counselors to make possible connections as we hear people's stories. It is even natural for us to make assumptions. But if we are not self-aware and fail to check our assumptions and instead proceed as if they're true, then we are not doing the harder work of knowing the person truly and accurately. If we aren't careful, we can begin to speak about our assumptions as if they are facts. We can believe there are problems that don't really exist. And if we begin to speak about them in that way, a counselee will feel missed and misunderstood.

CLOSURE LETTER

Finally, below is Nadia's closure letter. Notice how I reinforce aspects of her interpretation and imagined way forward. I cite a verse that we talked through together. I express trust in the Lord's faithfulness. As I said in chapter 13, these are similar to components I include in the last session, and a letter is a way for people to keep your words with them. Occasionally, I give the person the letter in the last session, instead of mailing it later. And sometimes I even read it aloud before giving it to the person to take.

***

Dear Nadia,

Now that our season of counseling has come to a close, I wanted to reach out and share a few thoughts that stand out from getting to know you and working with you.

Nadia, it was such a joy and privilege to meet you, hear your story, and walk with you. I know the panic you were experiencing at work was frightening and overwhelming, and I saw you leaning into the Lord for strength and help. I admired that.

I was also encouraged by your desire to grow in understanding how you could bring your faith to bear in addressing your panic. The Lord has compassion on you in your weaknesses, and he does not disdain your need for him. It is good to need him—and I saw you journey to seeing the beauty of that, and that it's more than okay to be dust when you have a strong Father who cares for you (Psalm 103:13–14). I trust you will continue to find him strong and true in your need.

Should you ever want to resume counseling, please do not hesitate to reach out. I'd welcome the opportunity to work with you again. CCEF would also be glad to assist you if you are ever in need of a referral to another source.

Blessings to you in Christ.

Sincerely,
Lauren Whitman

Chapter 15

CONSIDERATIONS AT THE END

Once the counseling process with the person has ended, take some time to reflect on the case. The following are some questions to prime the pump:

1. *What did you learn about God*—how he meets people, how he confronts, consoles, and cheers his children?
2. *What did you learn about people—about our condition?* What did you learn about the experience of living in a world like ours, with the problems we encounter, the struggles we have, and the limitations we face?
3. *What did you learn about yourself?* What are you good at, what is hard for you, what kinds of assumptions do you tend to make? As we said earlier, growing in self-understanding helps us love, and that will help us counsel in more effective ways.
4. *What Scripture passages or biblical truths were helpful for this person?* Think about whether further applications of those passages and truths could be made to other counseling cases and different concerns.

5. *What would you do again in future cases because it proved helpful in this case?* Our case wisdom benefits future counselees and our colleagues.

6. *Is there anything you did in this case that you wouldn't do again?* Along those same lines, if you could have a do-over of something you said or did with this counselee, what would you do differently and why? Failures and missteps also add to our case wisdom.

Afterword

A PROMISE FOR YOU, COUNSELOR

This book has laid out the process that we aim for as biblical counselors. The process shows us that the Lord entrusts us with a great responsibility. We are responsible to love people well and represent God in ways that bring glory and honor to his name. And the process shows us that we have a great privilege. If you ever ask biblical counselors what they love about what they do, one of the first responses you'll probably hear is that it is a privilege to be invited into someone's story. And it is. It is such a privilege.

As we think about the responsibility that we have to represent the Lord well, and the privilege we have to enter people's stories for their good, let me leave you with a promise: *counselor, you have a Counselor*. It's hard to imagine doing the work of counseling without the Lord, and thankfully we don't have to imagine that. What we do have to reckon with is a world that is painfully damaged. We have to reckon with the weight and burden of personal sin—in ourselves and in others. We have to reckon with the powers and authorities of evil, the principalities and systems of darkness (Ephesians 6:12).

Because of these realities, people are more complex than they are simple. Problems are more complex than they are simple. This is true of you, and it's true of me—and of everyone you will counsel. Complexities can be overwhelming, and it is easy to become overwhelmed as a counselor when we encounter people with problems that are immense and concerns that are not easily alleviated.

For those times, brothers and sisters, take comfort that your God is the first Counselor, the preeminent Counselor, the perfect Counselor. Isn't it interesting that one of his names is Wonderful Counselor (Isaiah 9:6)? His names are personal—and they connect to our personal needs. We need a Counselor, and we have what we need in him.

This also means he has gone before us in this work of counseling. And he promises this:

> I will instruct you and teach you in the way you should go; I will counsel you with my eye upon you (Psalm 32:8).

This verse has a broad-range application to our lives. Surely, God instructs and teaches us in all areas of life. He gives wisdom generously (James 1:5). But let's apply it to our work as biblical counselors.

- There is a way we should go as we walk with others—and with God's help we will find it.
- His loving eye is on us. Let's look to him—because he is looking at us.
- He knows we need his counsel to do our work—and so he supplies it.

FURTHER RESOURCES

- The search feature at ccef.org yields a wealth of free resources, including blogs, a podcast, and videos.
- For help with suicide assessment: Aaron Sironi and Michael R. Emlet, "Evaluating a Person with Suicidal Desires," *Journal of Biblical Counseling* 26, no. 2 (2012): 33–41.
- For thoughts on how to start a session: David Powlison, "Taking the Initiative in Counseling Ministry," *Journal of Biblical Counseling* 31, no. 2 (2017).
- When you wonder if someone really is ready to change: Todd Stryd, "How Do You Know If Someone Is Ready to Change?" *Journal of Biblical Counseling* 34, no. 2 (2020).
- For incorporating the whiteboard in a session to help people make connections: Todd Stryd, "Ode to the White Board: Helping People Make Connections," *Journal of Biblical Counseling* 30, no. 3 (2016): 68–84.
- For thinking about how God uses fallen people to help other fallen people: Todd Stryd, "God's Providence and Human Agency in Counseling," *Journal of Biblical Counseling* 33, no. 3 (2019): 41–57.

- To grow in using Scripture in counseling: Michael R. Emlet, *Cross Talk: Where Life and Scripture Meet* (Greensboro, NC: New Growth Press, 2009).
- For examples of using Scripture creatively and applied to specific counseling problems: see the "More Than a Proof Text" articles in the *Journal of Biblical Counseling*. They begin in volume 29, issue 1 (2015), and thirteen articles have been published to date.
- For counseling people who do not have faith in Christ: Alasdair Groves, "How Do You Counsel Non-Christians?" *Journal of Biblical Counseling* 26, no. 3 (2012).
- When you are looking for a topical resource to recommend to your counselee that you can then use in counseling as a jumping-off point for relevant conversations, see the 31-Day Devotionals for Life series by P & R Publishing that contains books on counseling topics. The series includes my book, *A Painful Past: Healing and Moving Forward*, and others that address a wide range of issues, including pornography, anger, chronic pain, toxic relationships, and many more.
- For providing support to a counselee who is taking psychoactive medications: Benjamin Crawford, "How to Help Counselees with Psychoactive Medications," *Journal of Biblical Counseling* 28, no. 2 (2014).
- For thinking biblically about how sanctification works: see David Powlison's book, *How Does Sanctification Work?* (Wheaton, IL: Crossway, 2017).
- For how to use homework in counseling: Robyn Huck, "Effective Homework in Counseling," *Journal of Biblical Counseling* 27, no. 1 (2013).

- For issues of domestic abuse:
  - Darby Strickland, *Is It Abuse?: A Biblical Guide to Identifying Domestic Abuse and Helping Victims* (Phillipsburg, NJ: P & R Publishing, 2020).
  - Search Leslie's Vernick's vast body of work at leslievernick.com.
- For ethical questions and considerations—for example, *Should I refer my counselee?*—it is important to be familiar with a code of ethics to help you think well about the matter.
  - See the American Counseling Association for their code at https://www.counseling.org/Resources/aca-code-of-ethics.pdf.
  - The American Association of Christian Counselors has a code as well: https://aacc.net/wp-content/uploads/2020/06/AACC-Code-of-Ethics-Master-Document.pdf.
- For an in-depth theological look at many of topics I've covered, including redemptive relationships, understanding the human heart, and the role of a biblical counselor: Paul David Tripp, *Instrument's in the Redeemer's Hands: People in Need of Change Helping People in Need of Change* (Phillipsburg, NJ: P & R Publishing, 2002).

ACKNOWLEDGMENTS

CCEF's collegial, collaborative environment has helped to make this book possible. Thank you to the entire counseling ministries team: I have been sharpened by every single one of you. Being a member of this team during the past ten years has been a constant source of learning and inspiration to me. Thank you to Cecelia Bernhardt for the faithfulness in how she leads our team. Thank you to Julie Lowe and Todd Stryd, who have overseen my counseling the most over the years. I feel particularly indebted to you both for the ways you have guided and informed my counseling practice. And thank you both for your input on this book. Julie, for patiently listening as I read portions aloud to you, and for thinking through subtle nuances with me! Todd, for talking through the table of contents with me at a critical point in my writing process. Thank you to Mike Emlet for your time and investment in this book. Your feedback on the drafts was gold.

Thank you to the counselees who have entrusted their stories to me. It is my honor and joy to have walked with each of you, and I am so grateful to God to know you and to have had fellowship in Christ with you.

Thank you to Barbara Juliani, who brainstormed with me what this book could become and believed that I could get it there.

Finally, this book is dedicated to my husband, Chad. Writing a book in a pandemic, while also working and homeschooling, felt impossible. Chad made it possible.

Christian Counseling & Educational Foundation

CCEF's mission is to restore Christ to
counseling and counseling to the church
by thinking biblically about the issues
of living in order to equip the church to
meet counseling-related needs.